the little book of
self-
soothing

the little book of

self-soothing

150 Ways to Manage Emotions, Relieve Stress, and Restore Calm

Robin Raven

Adams Media

New York London Toronto Sydney New Delhi

Adams media

Adams Media
An Imprint of Simon & Schuster, Inc.
100 Technology Center Drive
Stoughton, Massachusetts 02072

First Adams Media hardcover edition January 2023

ADAMS MEDIA and colophon are trademarks of Simon & Schuster.

For information about special discounts for bulk purchases, please contact Simon & Schuster Special Sales at 1-866-506-1949 or business@simonandschuster.com.

The Simon & Schuster Speakers Bureau can bring authors to your live event. For more information or to book an event contact the Simon & Schuster Speakers Bureau at 1-866-248-3049 or visit our website at www.simonspeakers.com.

Manufactured in China

10 9 8 7 6 5 4 3 2 1

Library of Congress Cataloging-in-Publication Data
Names: Raven, Robin, author.
Title: The little book of self-soothing / Robin Raven.
Description: Stoughton, Massachusetts: Adams Media, 2023 | Includes index.
Identifiers: LCCN 2022014640 | ISBN 9781507219614 (hc) | ISBN 9781507219621 (ebook)
Subjects: LCSH: Emotions. | Emotions--Problems, exercises, etc. | Stress management.
Classification: LCC BF561 .R38 2023 | DDC 152.4--dc23/eng/20220506
LC record available at https://lccn.loc.gov/2022014640

ISBN 978-1-5072-1961-4
ISBN 978-1-5072-1962-1 (ebook)

This book is dedicated to Joyce Houser, MFT.

Joyce, you're a shining, creative force for good in the world! Thanks for inspiring me on my journey of self-love and self-soothing.

contents

body 19

mind 77

spirit 135

introduction

Self-soothing is the process of taking immediate actions to help you feel better in this exact moment. It addresses your physical, mental, spiritual, and emotional needs to help you reduce everyday stresses, quiet the noise around you, and regain a sense of calm. Whether you just got bad news, feel anxiety creeping in, or are overstimulated after being in a loud group, it's important to learn self-soothing techniques that you can call upon to restore your physical and emotional health.

The Little Book of Self-Soothing is your guide to calming yourself when your body or the environment around you feels uncomfortable, unpleasant, or overwhelming. Like self-care and self-healing, self-soothing empowers you to take control of your situation and give your body what it needs in the moment. Though they are complementary, self-soothing differs from both self-care and self-healing. Self-care refers to the daily habits and actions you do to keep yourself mentally, physically, and spiritually healthy, while self-healing is more about long-term actions and things like seeing a therapist to heal from trauma. All three of these types of self-awareness are an important part of overall well-being.

The ideas and suggestions in this book will help you assemble a tool box of self-soothing techniques. Each of the three main sections—body, mind, and spirit—offers dozens of actionable ways to soothe yourself, whether in the short or long term. With these activities, you'll be able to support your overall well-being and health when you need a helping hand. For example, you'll:

* Go for a Walk in Nature
* Try Paired Muscle Relaxation
* Transform Judgmental Thoughts
* Let Go of False Worries
* Visualize a Treasure Chest of Comforts
* Detox Your Spirit

You can do most of these 150 exercises whenever you need to soothe yourself, whether you are at home, at work, or even on the go.

If you like, you can start at the beginning of the book and try a different self-soothing exercise any time you need it, or you can look through the contents to find an exercise that resonates with you at any particular moment. You might consider keeping a companion journal to this book so that you can write about what your feelings are before, during, and after each exercise. This record can help you identify the techniques that work best for you.

This book can empower you at every step of your self-soothing journey. These exercises and ideas will remind you to check in with your body and feelings during difficult moments and take action to recover your inner and outer peace. As you feel yourself move from agitated, tense, and upset to cool, calm, and collected, you will reclaim your sense of balance and well-being. Let *The Little Book of Self-Soothing* help you face life's ups and downs with confidence, composure, and grace.

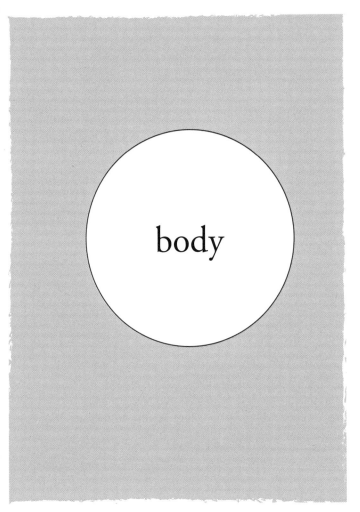

body

Relax with Aromatherapy

Aromatherapy is a holistic healing practice that uses scents to enhance your emotional and overall well-being. It can be especially helpful for self-soothing, as comforting and restful scents provide a calming atmosphere for you to breathe in and focus on.

Discovering which scents best soothe you will take a little trial and error. Start by gathering a variety of different essential oils. Consider popular ones like lavender, peppermint, rosemary, sweet orange, spearmint, pine, and cinnamon.

Now get a bunch of cotton rounds and sit down with your essential oils. Pour a couple of drops of one essential oil onto a cotton round. Hold it about six inches from your nose. Close your eyes and gently breathe in through your nose. Hold it closer if needed. Do you feel energized or calmed? Write down how that scent makes you feel.

Wait a few minutes, then repeat the practice for each of your chosen scents. After you try them all, look over your notes and decide which ones you want to use regularly for self-soothing.

Let Music Move Your Body

Getting your body in motion can actually calm and soothe your mind. How? When you're doing something fun that requires focus, it's easier to let go of anxiety, at least for a little while.

Start by turning on a song that usually inspires joy. Now close your eyes. Focus on the music and how you want to move your body. Imagine the music as a physical force touching your feet, ankles, legs, thighs, pelvis, stomach, midriff, chest, arms, shoulders, neck, face, and scalp. How do the parts of your body want to respond to the music? Trust your instincts. For example, do your feet want to tap to the music? Do they want to jump or spin instead? Move your feet however feels best to you.

How about your legs? Perhaps your legs want to glide across the floor, pretending that you're an ice dancer. Get your legs and feet working together with the music.

Now bring in your whole body. Throw your arms up in the air. Twist and turn from your waist. Bop your head to the beat if you're inspired to do so. Do any movements you'd like as long as you are engaging your whole body.

When the song ends, rest and reflect on how the dancing soothed you. Then put on another song and repeat the activity or just relax and revel in the moment.

Hold Your Heart While Humming

Your heart is the emotional center of your body. Focusing on it can be soothing and empowering, and this exercise may also inspire greater feelings of love for yourself.

First, get as comfortable as you can. Once you feel physically relaxed, place your hand on your heart and start to hum. Keep humming for about ten seconds, then pause.

Take your hand off your heart. Check in with yourself and assess the physical sensations you feel right now.

Now place your hand gently on your heart again and start humming. Hum for as long as it feels comfortable. As you do, think about the love that you have for yourself. If you aren't feeling love for yourself in this moment, act "as if" and pretend that you do.

Take a break, then once again put your hand over your heart and start humming. Envision love radiating from your heart and through your body, then try to visualize sending that love into the world. Remind yourself of all the power and love that you carry within you.

Be a Sloth

Soothe yourself by getting in touch with your inner sloth. In addition to being adorable, sloths are known for moving very slowly—in stark contrast to the rapid pulse of modern society that causes humans to rush through our lives.

For the moment, reject society's fast-paced pressures. Instead, slow down and behave as though you were a sloth. It's okay to feel silly at first. Embrace that!

To start, take a stance that helps you feel the most sloth-like. Perch on a sofa as though it's a tree or lie down on your stomach. Now go from the top of your head to the tips of your toes, making slow movements as a sloth might. Blink like a sloth might blink. Turn your head to the left and right with exaggerated slowness. Move your arms as slowly as you can.

Put all your focus into behaving like a sloth. It can be both distracting and soothing to immerse yourself in imaginative play like this. The relaxing pace of sloth behavior really inspires your body and mind to embrace calm.

Do a Mindful Food Tasting

Your senses hold the key to self-soothing on a very deep level. Tuning in to your senses encourages mindfulness, which is a powerful soothing technique. For this exercise, we'll delve into your senses of taste and smell.

Gather a couple of bites of five different snacks that you enjoy. They could be carrot sticks, a spoonful of peanut butter, a couple of potato chips, a small handful of walnuts, or any other snack. Place all five snacks on a plate and grab a spoon if it's needed. Bring your snack bites someplace where you can get very comfortable.

Now pick up one of the snacks and close your eyes. Try to put all previous experiences with the food aside for the moment. Bring the snack to your nose and breathe deeply a few times. Take in the scent as much as you can and think about what you can tell by the smell of the food. If you'd never tried it before, could you tell whether it's sweet or salty? What kind of feelings does the smell evoke in you? Does the scent alone bring back good or bad memories? Does the aroma make you hungry?

Next, take a bite and try to savor each taste sensation that you experience. Consider how much you think the food's smell influenced how it tastes. Consider whether the fragrance alone influenced your decision about the snack. Smell the next bite of the same snack while you're chewing. Does the way the food smells to you change now that you're eating it?

Repeat this process for all five snacks, taking sips of water between if needed. In addition to immediately soothing you, these focused sensory experiences with your food can help you be more mindful when you eat in the future.

Explore Circular Self-Massage

Massages are popular around the world in many different cultures because human touch is powerful and profound. Circular self-massage is just what it sounds like—a gentle massage using only small, circular motions.

To try this massage, start with your head. Put the tips of your fingers on each side of your temples and move them in a small, circular motion. Apply the level of pressure that feels best to you. As you massage, deeply inhale and exhale.

Now slowly massage your scalp. Move slowly back, up, across, and down until you have massaged your entire scalp. Next, move down to your neck. Continue the circular motions, paying attention to the signals your body is giving you and adjusting the pressure as needed.

Keep slowly massaging your body in a circular motion, going down over your shoulders, then down and up the length of each arm. Massage the length of your body down to your feet. Try to stay mindful of the soothing sensations you're experiencing in each moment.

Stand In Your Power

Your power as a human being isn't tied to your bank account, looks, or status in society. No matter what, you have a power that nobody can take away from you, and remembering and savoring that is an instant soothing balm.

Try to practice standing in your power right now. Close your eyes and imagine that you are a majestic mountain. Nothing can rattle you. Nothing can disturb the peace of the bold mountain. It is stronger than whatever might come at it, and the same is true for you.

As you visualize, consider what power truly means to you. How do you want to use the power that you have? Who or what besides yourself can benefit from your power?

Write down what it means to you to stand in your power, and try to stay in that frame of mind through the rest of today. When you stand in your power and embrace your strength, you build self-confidence and resilience, which can calm you as you face life's inevitable challenges.

Take Up Space

People are often made to feel that they are taking up too much space. For example, there's the unhealthy societal expectation that we all need to be dieting and trying to change our body image, or we're told not to feel emotions too intensely, so we should try to demand less attention. If something or someone has made you feel that you need to shrink and take up less space, reject that notion as quickly as possible. Soothe yourself with this exercise, which turns that notion 180 degrees.

Sit down comfortably on a sofa or bed. Yawn and stretch. Elongate your arms until they are sprawled as far out in the space as you can get them. Now lie down, stretching your arms and legs out as far as they can go.

Consider how calming and empowering it can be to stretch yourself to take up as much space as possible. While you probably can't do this easily in public, you can still call to mind the emotions this exercise evoked whenever someone wants you to be smaller in some way. It's a great way to give yourself permission to be as big and bold as you want to be.

Purse Your Lips

Pursing your lips can strengthen your relaxation techniques because it increases your focus and helps clear your mind of worries as you concentrate. Being more aware of your connection to your lips can help with mindfulness throughout the day.

Start this exercise by sitting in a comfortable spot. Inhale deeply for a few seconds. Now purse your lips as though you were going to blow out a candle or whistle a tune. Keep them pursed as you exhale for four to five seconds.

Repeat this exercise at least five times in a row. You may choose to continue for longer. As you inhale and exhale, try to be physically and mentally present in the moment and aware of what is going on in your body. Allow any feeling that pops up to simply be, and keep refocusing on your breath and body.

Describe the Textures

A heightened awareness of the texture of things can be a great way to shift your focus to the present moment, calm yourself, and allow you to see everyday items in a new way. To start this exercise, gather a few natural things such as a leaf, a pine cone, a clover, or a flower. Next, gather a variety of fabrics from your closet and a piece of paper and writing utensil.

Now sit down with all the things you gathered. Close your eyes and reach for one of the items. How soon could you tell what it was? Does it feel pleasant when you can't see it? What would you think it was if you had not been able to see it?

Now focus entirely on the item's texture. What does that feel like?

After you feel each item, write down your observations on its physical texture. Also record how the physical texture is soothing. If it reminds you of something, is the memory soothing?

This simple exercise lets your sense of touch lead the way as you concentrate on the here and now.

Observe the Fluidity of Movement

Have you ever noticed how fluid and soothing the movement of the human body can be? Some types of dance feature movements that can resemble gentle waves lapping upon the beach. Stand and try to move your body with that kind of graceful fluidity. After all, most of the human body is made of water!

Start with your arms. Using slow, smooth motions, wave your right arm up and down, then do the same for your left arm. Imagine each arm is water sloshing back and forth, then repeat the movements for both arms again.

Now sit down and add leg movements. Try to move your right leg up and down in a fluid way. Move your right arm and leg together from a seated position. Can you move them in sync as though they are a fluid moving as one? Try this with your left arm and leg.

Observe the fluidity of your movements. Allow them to fully soothe you and ground you in the beauty of the moment.

Do a Full-Body Scan

Conducting a careful review of how you are feeling physically and mentally in this moment can soothe you in a way few things can. A full-body scan can also soothe you because you are showing yourself that you are important and worthy of care. Try it for yourself to see how it can transform the way you're feeling.

Lie down in a place that you're most comfortable, then take a few deep breaths. Ask yourself what you are most aware of in this moment. Say it aloud. Do this for a few minutes, listing a new awareness each time if needed.

Now close your eyes and focus on your head. What are you aware of about your mind? How about your scalp and hair? What physical sensations are you aware of?

Now move to your face. Do you feel any sensations? Try licking your lips and assess how that makes you feel. Wrinkle your nose, then relax all the muscles in your face. Observe how you feel now.

Next, move to your neck and then your chest. Take a deep breath in and see how your chest rises. Move your awareness to your arms, then up to your shoulders and around to your back. Take in each physical sensation as it comes.

Continue now to your abdomen, midriff, stomach, and then your thighs and legs. Extend this down to your feet. Roll your feet around, thinking about all that they do to move you through life. Take this awareness of how you feel and allow it to fully soothe your body and mind.

Engage In Deliberate Breathing

Deliberate breathing can help fight stress both in the moment and over time. It can be soothing because it allows you to feel more in harmony with your body instead of like you're fighting it as you deal with shallow breathing and tense muscles.

Start by sitting in a comfortable spot and relaxing your body. If that means leaning back on a sofa or even lying down in bed, that's perfectly fine.

Now start observing your breathing. Notice how your body naturally moves when you breathe. Observe how your chest moves and how your belly rises and falls. Notice how breathing is affecting your body.

Now prepare to breathe more deliberately. Count to five or six as you inhale, then exhale to the count of five or six. Do this a few times in a row. Observe whether doing so changes anything in how your body is reacting. Then rest your body and try to relax your mind for a minute.

Now start again, inhaling for five seconds and then exhaling for five seconds. Try to continue deep breathing for at least a couple of minutes.

Touch Your Toes

Simple physical movement can sometimes distract your body from any emotional woes and provide powerful, soothing sensations. Stretching is an easy physical movement that can loosen tight muscles *and* help you overcome stress.

To test your ability to touch your toes, sit down on an exercise mat with your legs straight in front of you. Reach toward your toes. If you can't reach your toes, that's perfectly fine! The important thing is to gently stretch.

Now try an exercise that's sometimes called the windmill. Stand with your legs about a foot apart. Lift your right arm above your head, then bring it down to try to touch the toes of your left foot. Repeat this process with your left arm above your head, then bring it down to try to touch the toes of your right foot.

If you can't reach your toes in this position, that's fine too. Simply stretch as far as you comfortably can. This will help exercise several muscles in your body, including the hips and hamstrings. Try stretching at least three times per week for consistent self-soothing.

Swap the Sounds

When you get stressed out, even little things can get on your nerves. Soothe yourself by taking ownership of the things you can control. And a lot more is in your control than you might realize! For example, the sounds you hear around you are often largely within your control.

Start where you are and listen to the sounds that surround you. Do any of the sounds frustrate you? If so, try to swap them for ones you like. For example, if the sound of the washing machine is irksome to you, try to go to a different area of the house and turn on soothing music to drown out that sound. Phone notifications too annoying? Change them to a soothing chime. If you don't like the sound of a shutter flapping in the wind, secure it and then savor the silence.

Practice this with each room of your home. Swap sounds you dislike for ones that you love. As you do this, try to revel in the power you have to make your environment more pleasant and inviting.

Wrap Yourself in Warmth

When the weather is chilly, few things feel quite as good as sitting by a fire or wrapping yourself in a nice, warm blanket. This soothing practice can help you unwind more fully as you relax into the warmth.

Set the temperature to be cool in your home, then turn on a heated blanket. Let it warm up for five minutes, then lie down and wrap it fully around you. Once the warm blanket is completely wrapped around you, you might feel a little bit like a human burrito, but you should also feel the wonderful sensations of warmth.

Get completely comfortable while you remain wrapped in the blanket's warmth. Stay in the moment and focus your mind on all the physical sensations that are happening with your body. What does the blanket feel like against your skin? How does it alter the way you were feeling emotionally? Savor the warmth.

Breathe Into Your Belly

The belly is a wonderful part of the human body, yet a lot of people feel self-conscious about theirs. Use this exercise to take time to appreciate your belly and all it does for you. It's beautiful and strong, and practicing deep-belly breathing can be incredibly soothing.

To prepare, lie down on your back and bend your knees, keeping your feet on the floor. Get comfortable, then place your right hand on your belly and your left hand on your heart. Your left hand will remain still during this exercise, but your right hand will rise and fall with your breaths.

Slowly breathe in deeply, imagining your breath going directly to your belly. As you take in the deep breath, your belly will rise. Exhale as you slowly squeeze your abdominal muscles. Repeat this practice several times until you feel calmed and relaxed.

This type of breathing helps slow down the pace of your breathing. It takes less energy to breathe in this way, so it's good practice for when you need to catch your breath too.

Chew Three Pieces of Gum

It's not usually a great idea to use food to self-soothe unless you do it mindfully, as in the Do a Mindful Food Tasting exercise in this chapter. Chewing gum can offer delightful tastes without interfering with a healthy diet.

Grab a pack of gum in your favorite flavor. Close your eyes and taste the gum. Chew it and savor the taste. How long does the flavor last? When it starts to fade, add a second piece of gum. When that flavor starts to fade, add a third piece of gum. When the taste of all three pieces fades, continue to chew only if the sensation of chewing without taste brings you pleasure.

Write down what the tastes made you feel. Now ask yourself whether the chewing itself was a positive experience. In what ways did it soothe you? Consider repeating this when you need to be soothed in the future, especially if you are on the go.

Do a Quick Succession
of Fast-Paced Moves

Remember when you were a kid and running around was just pure joy? Close your eyes and try to return to that frame of mind where you wanted to race and chase your friends for fun. That carefree and happy vibe of childhood can help soothe you when you have adult worries.

Go outside or choose a spot inside where there is a lot of space. Try to think only of the joy of movement and allow it to be a soothing force throughout your body and mind. To prepare, stretch for two minutes.

Now stay in the moment as you try this succession of fast-paced moves. Do twenty jumping jacks in a row. If you are tired, take a break. If not, go straight into running (in place, if necessary) as fast as you can for twenty seconds. Pause, then run for another twenty seconds. Try to do this ten times. Next, try skipping for thirty seconds. After that, try jogging in place for a minute. Then return to jumping jacks and start the sequence over. Repeat it three times or until you need a break.

Shut Out Distractions

When one of your senses is temporarily reduced, others feel sharpened, and this instant focus can provide an immediate sense of comfort too. For this exercise, try dwelling in darkness for a bit. You'll temporarily shut out whatever is stressing you so you can focus on calming yourself.

Start by getting a blindfold, then go to a safe, clean part of your home with a comfortable sitting area. Make sure there is nothing in the way that you could trip on. Now close all the curtains and turn off the lights.

Sit down and put on the blindfold. Close your eyes too. Pay attention to what you might imagine within the darkness. If problems come to mind, imagine them fading away into the darkness. Let them fall into a black hole one at a time until they no longer exist in this moment.

Keep the blindfold on but open your eyes. Consider whether anything changed in your vision. Do you feel okay, or is this uncomfortable? What feelings does this darkness inspire?

Now take off the blindfold. Since the curtains are closed and the lights are off, it should still be fairly dark. How do your eyes feel as they adjust to a low level of light?

Now walk around carefully, exploring how different it is to walk with little light. Turn the lights back on. As you do so, imagine all your worries fading away with the darkness.

Go for a Walk in Nature

Few things are as restorative to your mind, body, and spirit as experiencing the true beauty of nature. Take the time to go for a short, soothing walk in the great outdoors. Keep it simple; you don't have to go on an ambitious hike. A stroll through a local park or even your backyard works well for this exercise.

As you walk, try to focus entirely on what is around you. Take note of the sights. What is most beautiful here? Can you tell how old the trees are? Can you spot any wildlife? (Adorable squirrels totally count!)

Now take in the smells. Can you identify any scents that you really like? Now reach out and touch a leaf on a tree or a flower. Did it feel like you thought it would?

Finally, turn around slowly. How does the view change as you turn?

When you are done, observe how being outside in the natural world can quiet a noisy mind.

Take a Sensory Bubble Bath

Bubble baths are the go-to self-soothing solution for many people. That makes sense because the warm water soothes aching muscles and the quiet luxury can calm your mind. Plus, if you have a tub, they're simple to enjoy. For a truly special experience, try this exercise to maximize your sensory experience.

Before you run the bath, choose a scented bubble bath or lotion. Fluff a clean towel in the dryer so it's warm to the touch. Finally, make yourself a mug of herbal tea to sip as you soak.

Set aside an hour when you can block out all distractions, then fill the tub. Now it's bath time. Listen to the gentle sounds of lapping water, look at all the bubbles, taste your tea, smell the scented products, and when you're done, enjoy how the warm towel feels against your skin. Let each aspect of the bath you've chosen be a soothing sensory experience.

Listen to Yourself

Many of us turn to someone else's voice when we want to be soothed—a beloved singer, a calm podcast, or a favorite TV show. But when you want to self-soothe, your own voice can be just as reassuring. In this exercise, you'll appreciate your voice for all that it allows you to convey and communicate to yourself and others. Consider how you can soothe and comfort yourself with your own singing or by saying the right thing at the right time.

To start, listen to the sound of your own voice as you hum. Then listen to yourself talk aloud about whatever is on your mind. Get it all out. In what ways is your voice beautiful? Do your best to appreciate the qualities that make your voice unique and special.

Now close your eyes and listen to the sound of your voice as you sing. Think about all the things you like about your voice. Then open your eyes and write down what you appreciate about it. Revel in its power to soothe you.

Appreciate Your Hands

It's easy to take your hands for granted, even though they do a million useful tasks to keep things running smoothly in your life. Your hands are a great source of power too. Today, they can help soothe you.

Sit at a desk or table, and place both hands in front of you on the hard surface. Pull your fingers into tight fists, hold them for three seconds, then release your hands. Repeat this five times.

Rest your hands, palms up, for five seconds. Look at the physical shape of your hands, including all your fingers. Focus on gratitude for all your hands empower you to do. Now use your right hand to massage the inner palm of your left hand for thirty seconds. Focus on the pleasant sensations. Now massage your right palm with your left hand.

Focus on how you can soothe one hand with the other, and how you can soothe yourself with your own hands. Celebrate the power and strength in each hand.

Make Funny Faces

Humor and silliness can take your mind off more serious worries, even if just temporarily. In that spirit, embrace your inner child for this exercise. Sit down in front of a mirror and loosen up the muscles in your face and shoulders.

Look in the mirror and try to keep a straight face as you scrunch up your nose and stick out your tongue. If laughter comes, embrace it. Next, try to raise your eyebrows high while exaggerating a frown with your lips. See how contorted your facial features can be, then hold it for three seconds while observing yourself in the mirror. Then rest your features as your face returns to normal.

Next, think of the funniest face you ever made at someone when you were a kid. Try to re-create that now as you look in the mirror. Did you crack yourself up? Why or why not?

By making silly faces in the mirror, you can distract yourself from your problems while soothing yourself with some basic, natural humor.

Sing a Meaningful Song

There's just something about belting out a favorite tune that helps you process your feelings and change your whole outlook. Choose a song that has great purpose and meaning to you. It can be a song that is passionate about goodness or one that effectively releases a great deal of pain.

Listen to the song you chose and try to sing along as you do. Don't worry about getting the lyrics down perfectly or hitting every note right. The important part of this exercise is to be in tune to the feeling that the song represents. Allow the song to empower you to release that feeling from within yourself.

Once you get out the feeling you're experiencing in the moment, reflect on the soothing power of both happy and sad songs. Consider which type is most soothing to you so that you know whether to reach for an upbeat or a reflective song to help calm you down the next time you need it.

Savor a Nurturing Meal

While you don't want to get in the habit of using food as a reward, eating a delicious, nutritious meal can be soothing and pleasurable—and it's something you should do every day anyway. Planning a nourishing meal is a great way to soothe and take care of yourself.

Start by choosing healthy foods that you truly love. Whether you want to start with an ingredient (perhaps black beans to serve as the base for vegan chili?) or you think of a whole meal (maybe a plant-based frozen meal that takes five minutes to microwave), try to focus on vegetables, fruits, and healthy proteins. Opting for healthy food that tastes great offers you immediate comfort and enjoyment, while also being good for your long-term health.

Set aside at least half an hour to enjoy your meal once you've prepared it. Get rid of all the usual distractions and focus on savoring each bite. Consider all the senses that are sated and soothed while you are eating. Your senses of sight, hearing, smell, touch, and of course taste can be delighted by a great meal.

Do a Victory Dance

We've all seen athletes celebrate a score with a victory dance. Well, victory dances can also take your mind off a difficult subject and place it on all the wins in your life. In this exercise, you'll comfort and soothe yourself by honoring your victories instead of ruminating on your worries.

First, think of something worth celebrating, keeping in mind that it can be something big or small. It could be a recent accomplishment at work, hitting a milestone in a hobby, starting therapy, or finishing a paper by a deadline. It should feel like a big deal to you. Let the joy it brings be an initial soothing balm as you further move your focus to the victory dance.

Now turn on a celebratory, upbeat song and start moving your body. Don't judge yourself or think about how the dance would look to others. This is just for you. You can kick your legs up, do a little shuffle, or move your body in any way that feels good to you. The important thing is to simply get moving.

With each move, focus on the emotions you're feeling. Think about how you originally felt when whatever you're celebrating happened. Relish that this is *your* moment. Close your eyes briefly and relive the pleasure of the victory if you need to re-center your focus during the dance.

If you want, create a whole routine to celebrate your victory. Savor the soothing and confidence-building feelings that come up as you recognize your achievement with happy movements.

Draw on Yourself

Your body is a masterpiece and a work of art. Celebrate a part of your body that you love by drawing on it with a skin-safe temporary marker. If you don't want others to see it, draw on a part of your body that you can easily cover up with clothing. This exercise is soothing as it focuses your attention on creating and offers the instant reward of seeing the art on your skin. The physical sensation of writing on your skin might also feel calming.

The drawing can be as simple or complex as you want. If you don't like to draw or don't feel confident doing so, simply make a circle and write a meaningful phrase inside it. You might choose to write your name, the name of a loved one, or an uplifting phrase that always makes you feel better.

Take a selfie of the drawing so that you can look at it again when you need a little lift. Then keep the drawing on your skin for as long as you feel comfortable. If you want to wash it away immediately, that's okay too. The important part is to focus on how soothing it is in the moment.

Skip for Joy

Physical movement can have a very big impact on how you feel. In fact, it is a scientifically proven mood booster. Physical activity can soothe anxious feelings, and this exercise is all about being soothed by the joy of movement.

Which movement is more joyful than the simple act of skipping? Most kids enjoy skipping as part of regular play. There's no reason why adults shouldn't embrace this joyful movement as well.

Go to an area where you have plenty of space, whether it's an open spot where you exercise or your backyard. Start skipping in a large circle. Keep going until you feel you need to take a break. It's okay if that is ten seconds or ten minutes. Be gentle with yourself.

Take a break and reflect on how you feel. Do you feel a sense of relief or calm?

Now try skipping again. With each movement, think of something that brings you joy. Connect the merry movements with happy thoughts.

Rest again and reflect on the soothing sensation you feel. Write about these feelings.

Reset Your Sense of Taste

Your senses are significantly affected by what has previously happened. That's why chefs may provide palate cleansers between courses. Your sense of taste is also influenced by what you smell and a vast variety of other things.

The sense of taste is complex, and it can be a strong, soothing force in your life. For this exercise, it's time to reset your sense of taste. While you don't want to use food to soothe yourself too often, this activity encourages slow, mindful eating.

Prepare a serving of your favorite food. Now sit down with your favorite food and spend a minute looking at it while savoring the way it smells. Take in a deep breath and focus on the joy of anticipation while thinking of the most appetizing way to describe the dish in words.

Take one bite and devour it slowly, taking in all the sensations it brings. Now brush your teeth, then drink a full glass of water. Eat a second bite. Do you notice anything different now?

Finally, take another small bite and savor it. Eat the whole serving slowly while savoring how pleasurable and soothing the sense of taste can be.

Try Paired Muscle Relaxation

Human beings are wonderfully complex. Our physical bodies are intertwined with our emotions in so many ways. That's why tension in your emotions often manifests as tension in your body. Muscle relaxation techniques can soothe both difficult emotions and the muscle strains that can accompany them.

In this exercise, you'll tense and relax different pairs of muscle groups, starting with your eyebrows and working your way down to your toes. Start by lying down on a bed or sofa. Get as comfortable as possible.

Raise both your eyebrows as high as you can and hold them there for five seconds, then release them and relax for twenty seconds. Next, close your eyes tightly for five seconds, then release them and relax for twenty seconds.

Pull up your shoulders and hold them for five seconds, then release them and relax for twenty seconds. Next, clench your hands for five seconds, then release them and relax for twenty seconds.

Next, clench your buttocks together for five seconds, then release and relax for twenty seconds.

Move to your thighs and clench them for five seconds, then release and relax for twenty seconds.

Point your toes toward your face for five seconds, then release and relax for twenty seconds. Next, point your toes away and curl them downward. Hold this position for five seconds, then release and relax for twenty seconds.

Now try to release all the stress and pressure in your entire body and lie limp for sixty seconds while breathing deeply in and out. Envision yourself releasing stress and tension with each exhale.

Freeze in Place

Going from movement to stillness very quickly can encourage you to take stock of your body in the present moment. Plus, keeping all your limbs perfectly still is more difficult than it seems—and the concentration it requires can help distract you from your worries.

Start by doing something you enjoy. Then, in the middle of doing it, stop as if you were in a film when someone hits the pause button. Whether you are in the middle of a dance move or cleaning your closet, freeze in place for thirty seconds. While you're still, try to clear your mind of all woes and worries. Breathe deeply and try to focus only on the stillness of your body and the physical challenge of the moment.

Now continue what you were doing for a minute, then pause again. Repeat the instructions from the previous paragraph.

When you release your body from the frozen position, sit down and relax. Reflect upon how it feels to be as still as possible.

Compliment Yourself

You probably see mirrors every day, but have you ever thought of them as a self-soothing tool? This activity might change your mind.

Clear a space in front of the largest mirror in your home. Now stand or sit in front of your mirror. Close your eyes for a few seconds, then open your eyes and look directly into your eyes. Try to look at them with pure self-love. If any criticisms come to mind, replace them with loving compliments.

Think of three positive adjectives that describe your eyes. Now look at your nose and mouth, then also think of adjectives that describe what you love the most about these features.

Turn to your side and look in the mirror. Now turn to the other side and look at your reflection. Turn with your back to the mirror, then look back at your reflection.

With every glance and movement, let loving compliments flood and soothe your mind.

Create Sounds for Each Emotion

Sometimes emotions can get confusing if multiple ones compete for prominence. For example, if something good happens, you may want to celebrate. However, some past issues may vie for your attention, reminding you of the ways that things went wrong before. Associating each emotion with a sound can help you sort out competing emotions and find peace on a spiritual level.

Start by creating a sound for a difficult feeling. Anger might have a growl associated with it. Think about how your emotion would sound if it had a voice.

Next, start creating sounds to represent the positive feelings that you have. They can be squeals of delight, humming, or any other pleasing sound.

Narrow your focus to one strong positive emotion that you are feeling. You don't have to deny the other emotions, but choosing to focus on one that's especially resonating with you can help center you. Now repeat the sound for that emotion several times in a row. See if repeating the basic sound of the emotion can help you stay in that state for a while.

Listen to Your Body's Complaints

It's very frustrating when people dismiss your medical concerns or try to deny thoughts you have or pain you feel. The thing is, you don't have to accept the negativity of these naysayers. Soothe yourself by learning to validate your own complaints and feelings.

Stand up and take an awareness of your body. Do any parts of your body feel sore, hurt, or uncomfortable? If so, consider whether you've sought help for the problem. If you haven't, make a note to seek help. If you have but weren't met with the response you want and need, reassure yourself by offering the response you deserved. Then also make a note to find a new doctor.

Soothe yourself by validating all the pain or discomfort you feel. Acknowledge it. Reassure yourself that you should have been seen and heard in the first place. See and hear the problem now. Promise yourself that you will fight for yourself and find solutions for any emotional and physical pain you have.

Savor Spices

All your senses are incredibly powerful. Taste can provide a lot of joy and comfort even if you're going through a difficult time. One healthy way to challenge and delight your sense of taste is to try different spices.

Select three spices you've never tried before. Read about them and learn their history and flavor profile, but don't do any taste testing. Now prepare an unseasoned dish, such as pasta or rice.

Divide the dish into three bowls, and season each with one of the three spices. Label each bowl in the back or on the bottom so you can't see it, then mix up the bowls until you no longer know which is which.

Close your eyes and try each different dish. Guess which one it is as you taste it, then see if you were right. Savor the spices in each dish and feel grateful for your senses and the comfort they can bring you.

Practice Your Listening Skills

The art of communication is complex because people have different ways of expressing (or not expressing) themselves. As a result, people often get hurt because of misunderstandings and miscommunication. If you're upset by a problem with communication, soothe yourself with the knowledge that misunderstandings are a normal part of life, and that you can improve how you communicate. The following exercise can help.

Choose three *YouTube* videos that are about a minute long, and watch all three in a row. Then think back to the first video. What was the first thing that the person said? In the second video, did the person have a deep voice or a high voice? Can you repeat anything word-for-word from the third video?

If you're like most people, you will have trouble answering those questions. But take heart, because you can improve with practice. Try three more videos but focus more on listening carefully.

Making any necessary improvements to your listening skills can make you feel calmer and more confident when you are communicating with others.

Time Your Movement

Timing repetitive movements can help you get your mind off anything stressful and instead focus on your body. This exercise is especially helpful if you don't have a lot of time to exercise right now.

Go for a short, leisurely walk. Set the timer on your phone to go off in one minute, then start your walk. Meanwhile, count the time in your head up to sixty seconds, trying to keep in perfect time so you reach sixty when the alarm goes off.

Now advance to running or walking very quickly for a minute, counting each second in your mind. Pause to relax, then go back to slower walking. Count another minute of walking.

Alternate between the two until you are tired. Then sit down and reflect on how different you feel after exercising with your mind occupied the entire time. It can be extremely soothing to work the body without giving your mind a chance to wander to worries.

Embrace Light and Shade

The splendor of light can offer an instant surge of cheer, while cool shade can also be immediately refreshing on a hot day. Savoring both light and shade can help you find ways to soothe yourself in either condition.

For this self-soothing exercise, go into your yard or a nearby park. Find a tree or other structure that offers a consistent, cooling shade.

Sit in the shade for a few minutes and spend time daydreaming or writing in a journal. Do your best to keep your mind on pleasant things. Then stop and look at the nearby light. What do you observe about it? From your point of view as you sit in the shade, what do you find desirable about the light?

Now stand and slowly step into the light while savoring all the sensations you feel along the way. Allow the sun to bathe you in warmth and soothe you with its comforting light.

Play with Puppets

The art of puppetry is a great way to express yourself in an art form that you may have never tried before. It may feel silly at first, but it can also be incredibly soothing to be so engaged in creativity.

Gather two old socks. Make simple faces on them with a marker. Give them names that represent two emotions that you struggle to express. For example, you may want to name one Joy and the other Anger.

Now put on a little puppet show for yourself. Let each puppet express whatever comes to your mind. If you have problems expressing your anger, let your angry puppet express all the things that fill you with rage. If you have issues expressing joy, think of the things that genuinely bring you happiness and let your puppet express them.

Now put the puppets aside and reflect on what you learned from expressing your emotions so freely. Let the release soothe you and inspire you to express yourself more fully. Return to put on a puppet show any time.

Act Out Words

Words are the cornerstone of most communication. Whether you are expressing your deepest joys or most outrageous frustrations, you probably rely on the power of words. The soothing power of language is also a vital part of helping yourself feel better when you need it.

For this exercise, grab a dictionary or open a dictionary app or website. Randomly go to a word, then look at and think about what that word means to you. Stand and act out that word for yourself for fifteen seconds. For example, if you got the word "statue," you might try to stand in your most stately pose.

Repeat this for a few more words, acting out each word for fifteen seconds. You may get stumped as you try to act out certain words. Just go with the flow and trust your instincts.

Now choose one specific word that always makes you feel better and act it out in a way that you find soothing. Revel in the power of this word.

Be Kind to Your Feet

Your feet get so much use—and sometimes abuse—every day. It's important to take the time to give your feet TLC each day. Doing so can offer relaxing, calm feelings to your whole body.

If possible, get into a warm bath and start by massaging your feet. You may use a favorite massage oil or a foot massager to assist you. Pay close attention to the most sensitive areas of your feet.

Rub the arches of your feet very gently. Bend your toes and massage them individually. Let your thumbs apply pressure to the center of each foot. Next, squeeze your heels and massage each foot's pressure points. Then wash both feet thoroughly with a moisturizing soap or body wash.

Dry your feet, making sure the areas between your toes get very dry, and sprinkle your feet with foot powder or antifungal powder. Coat them with lotion if desired. Put on comfortable slippers and savor the soothing sensation of freshly cared-for feet!

Focus On Your Peripheral Vision

Your peripheral vision is how you can see out of the corners of each eye. In order to see what's there, you need to slow down and be fully present in the moment. Pausing to see what's in your peripheral vision can refocus your body and mind on the here and now instead of on what's worrying you.

Start by going somewhere outside where there is something lovely to see with your peripheral vision in each eye. Try to choose a place where you aren't likely to be interrupted.

Practice staying focused on your peripheral vision as you blink your eyes quickly. What do you notice? Can you see any changes in the world around you as you blink quickly?

Now slow down the blinking to normal as you maintain a focus on your peripheral vision. What changes as you transition to a normal blinking pace? What do you notice? Have you noticed any birds flying or movements from a breeze?

Maintain a focus on your peripheral vision for at least one whole minute while you try to stay perfectly still and breathe deeply. Pay attention to what moves around you, if anything. What most catches your eye? Look for things in your peripheral vision that bring you joy.

Now roll your head in a circle while keeping that focus. Move your head from side to side and notice what changes in your peripheral vision. Carefully walk around while keeping that focus.

Note the joy and beauty you would have missed without this focus. Exploring your peripheral vision can help you soothe yourself by refocusing on the present moment and finding joy in the world around you.

Create a Self-Soothing Playlist

❋

Music is a wonderful way to escape or to savor the moment, depending on what you need. For this exercise, you'll make a self-soothing playlist to have a powerful tool you can come back to any time you need it.

Start by adding songs you know can soothe you. To round out the list, look at your favorite artist's lesser-known songs, or see if your music service recommends other artists with similar styles. You can also go in the other direction and add a few songs that you *don't* know well but that seem soothing. Go with what works for you without judgment. Trust yourself.

Your playlist may need to evolve over time. As you discover new music that calms you or remember old tunes you'd forgotten, feel free to adjust it. Also, it's okay to take music off the playlist any time you notice it no longer soothes you. This should be a continually evolving tool for soothing yourself in the good and bad times.

Change Up Your Hair

Are you ready to try something fun with your hair? Today is a day to have fun with it and let the physicality of a new style soothe your body, mind, and spirit. The simple act of styling your hair can be soothing.

First, decide what you want to do. Will you curl it, straighten it, color it, put it up, or let it down? Maybe it's more about what you *won't* do to your hair that will be different.

Once you've styled your hair the new way, look in the mirror. How does this make you feel? Whether or not you like the look and want to keep it, celebrate what is beautiful about the style.

Go On a Date with Yourself

If you learn to love your own company, you'll be better able to soothe yourself when you need comfort. For this exercise, you are going to put forth effort into being your own best company.

Think about what your ideal date would include. Pick a great restaurant and choose an activity that you like to do by yourself. It's okay if it's something as simple as going to the movies. You're not trying to impress anyone but yourself, so take the opportunity to do what you truly most want to do on a date.

Then set out to plan that experience for yourself. Don't invite a friend along. This date is meant to be totally solo.

Bring along a journal and write down your thoughts throughout the date. What do you want to say to yourself? Record the ways that this fun activity is soothing and entertaining.

Try Controlled Breathing

Controlled breathing can help you soothe and calm your-self anytime, anywhere. It encourages you to find power in controlling how you breathe, and being mindful of your body as you do.

Stand and take a deep breath in, then pause for at least five seconds. Exhale slowly. Repeat this five times in a row. A popular goal with controlled breathing is to take in only five breaths for a minute. So, try to do this until you can pause your breath for around ten seconds each time. Only hold your breath if you feel fully comfortable and stop if you don't feel good.

As you take each breath, imagine a soothing force coming over your body. The breaths should help you get and stay calm.

Massage Yourself with Ice in a Warm Bath

This self-soothing exercise will show you how becoming aware of your physical sensations can help calm your emotions. Start by preparing a warm bubble bath. Next, grab a cup of ice and a hand towel or facecloth, then sit down in the bath. Relax your neck and take a few deep breaths. Now wrap a couple of pieces of ice in the towel.

Close your eyes and slowly press the ice to your forehead. Stay focused on how the ice is making you feel. Rather than letting your mind wander to your worries, focus only on the ice.

Hold the ice to your forehead for three seconds, then slowly caress your entire forehead with it. Then, without taking the ice off your face, move down and around and caress your entire face with the ice. Pay attention to how it makes you feel. Does it shock your system? Does it make you feel refreshed? Does it feel pleasant or unpleasant?

Open the hand towel and add a few more pieces of ice, then wrap them up tightly. Now apply the ice to your neck. Circle your entire neck with the ice. Move back up, pressing the ice behind your ears and then to your scalp.

Slowly move the ice to the rest of your body, staying in the moment. Pay attention to how the ice makes you feel throughout the exercise. Notice how it is cooling and soothing in contrast to the warmth of the bathwater. Savor all the positive feelings it inspires.

Celebrate the Power of Your Body

The human body is an incredibly powerful force, and it can do things that scientists haven't yet even realized. For this exercise, let your body's power soothe and uplift you.

First, consider the types of energy that the human body uses and gives off. Power in the human body can come from muscles, but the body can also do things like warm someone else up if you snuggle with them. The human body can even power devices like bikes and crank radios.

Now get on a stationary bike or a real bike. Start moving your legs and powering the bike slowly, then visualize how you are responsible for generating power. Slowly gather speed and pay close attention to how the movement of your legs is affecting every other part of your body.

Now relax and write about how the physical motion of your body felt freeing and soothing.

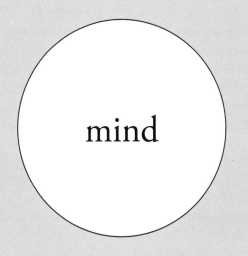

mind

Make a List of What's Bothering You

If you are stressed out, one of the best things that you can do to soothe yourself is free your mind of the worries bouncing around in your head. So, grab a sheet of paper or open a document on your computer.

Close your eyes for thirty seconds. Breathe in and out and consider everything that you are aware of in the moment. Now open your eyes and start writing down everything you are aware of. Do this without judgment of what you will see when you read it later. There should be no limits. Write down everything, from thoughts about what you want to eat for dinner tonight to serious big-picture things that keep you awake at night. As you write, focus your awareness on everything that is bothering you. Get it all out.

When you're done writing, close your eyes for another thirty seconds. Once again, breathe in and out. Become aware of what is most actively bothering you right now. It's likely that new thoughts will come to mind that you need to express. Grab a new sheet of paper or open a fresh document. Write down the things that are still bothering you. Write for as short or as long a time as you want. Just focus on expressing whatever comes to mind.

As you write down the things that are causing you stress, envision them leaving your mind and your body. They are now recorded elsewhere, so you don't have to keep them front of mind anymore. Try to imagine that they have gone somewhere else or disappeared entirely. Let your mind release those concerns and feel soothed.

Reassure Yourself

When times get tough, a little reassurance from others can go a long way. It's universally soothing to hear reminders that you are loved, valued, and needed. If you need to ask for reassurance, do so. The good news is that if you're alone or don't have anyone to talk to at the moment, you can reassure yourself too!

Reassuring yourself is a powerful self-soothing technique because you're showing yourself that you're worthy of love and care. Plus, practicing positive self-talk can help you build confidence and self-reliance. So, try to identify exactly which insecurities you are feeling in the moment and how you need reassurance. For example:

* If you feel overwhelmed, say something like, "This is really difficult, but I will make it through and feel great again."
* If you are in emotional pain, maybe say, "I am in so much pain, but it will heal. I am strong, and I am more than capable of surviving this pain. I will thrive."

Say these to yourself or aloud, or say whatever you need to hear in a kind and compassionate way. Let yourself be soothed by your thoughts. If you find any statements particularly helpful, write them down and reread them every time you need reassurance.

Plan a Trip

National Geographic reported that simply planning a trip can have a positive impact on your mental health. That's true regardless of whether the trip ultimately happens. Planning a vacation is soothing because it provides something concrete to look forward to. When you feel stressed or anxious about something, letting your mind wander to some future happiness encourages positivity and motivation.

Take the time to start planning a vacation you want to take. Choose somewhere you're excited to go and can visit within the next two years. Pick the specific destination and choose who you'd like to go with you. Getting others on board can enhance the excitement, and it can be fun to make plans together.

Next, work on a loose itinerary and figure out where you'll stay. Decide on restaurants where you'll dine. Pick adventures that you must experience. Start visualizing how these events might look and feel like. Add extra details like what you'd ideally wear and what the weather might be like.

Whenever you want some extra cheer in your life, continue researching and planning the trip. Imagine all the fun you'll have and savor that joy.

Write Five Sincere Compliments for Yourself

Loving yourself is a key part of overall well-being. Maintaining a great love for yourself will help you weather the inevitable storms that life hurls at all of us. Genuinely loving yourself can soothe you when things go wrong because you will have faith that you are strong enough to get through this tough time.

First, envision a space in your heart and mind where you hold love for yourself. Now think of and write down five things that you appreciate about yourself. Aim for a combination of physical features, key characteristics or traits, and goals you've achieved.

If you struggle to come up with compliments, try standing up and looking in the mirror. Write down something you find beautiful about yourself. Next, describe the last few goals you had that took persistence to achieve. Finally, consider adding compliments other people have given you recently.

As you write down each compliment, allow yourself to really feel the refreshing, soothing love you deserve!

Imagine Your Own Music Video

Music has a unique power to influence your thoughts and feelings, and you can harness its power for self-soothing too! This kind of visualization is great for soothing your mind because it can block worries for a while and inspire you to imagine fun, creative new things.

For this exercise, choose a song you love that can help you right now, whether you need to be calmed, energized, or uplifted. (Ideally, the song doesn't already have its own music video.) Play the song of your choice, then stretch and relax as you listen to it a few times.

Now, as the song starts over again, try to envision what its music video would be like if you directed it. Would you star in it? Does it have a storyline or special aesthetic? It's all up to you.

Start the song over when it finishes. This time, try to visualize the entire video you just created. Enjoy watching it play in your mind as fully as you can, focusing on all the little details.

Experience the Sensations of Safety

Feeling truly safe is a basic human need that provides a sense of calm in your life. If it is not too traumatic, think back to a time when you felt afraid, then consider the relieved emotions and feelings your mind enjoyed when you regained your sense of safety.

Close your eyes and try to relive that feeling in this moment. Sometimes going back and reliving powerful, positive emotions can bring instant comfort even many years after you initially had such feelings.

Now think about what safety means to you today. What do you need to feel physically, mentally, spiritually, and emotionally safe? Make a list of the things that pop into your head. If you can take quick actions to bring any of the things on the list to fruition, do them.

Once you've done all that you can immediately do to make yourself feel safe and sound, reflect on the sensation of security and imagine a feeling of soothing peace seeping through your veins and reaching your whole body.

Make the Moment a Little Better

Self-soothing isn't about pretending things are fine. This moment may not be good, and that's okay. Call it out for all the bad things that are happening right now. Try not to ignore or be afraid of them. It's okay to speak your fears and even write them down. Facing unpleasant truths is part of the journey to a place where you're truly soothed.

Now try to name all the things that you can do right now to make this moment even a little better. For example, if you are hot, try to cool down. See if that has an impact on your mood. Sometimes we don't realize the power we have to make simple changes that can calm and relax us.

Experiment with all sorts of things that come to mind about making this moment better. Take notes about what works and what doesn't. You can revisit your notes later to better soothe yourself, and you will save time by knowing what does and doesn't work.

Stand Up for Yourself

It can be hard to think on your feet and come up with comebacks when someone is mean to you. The best one-liners always seem to come to mind when it's too late to say them. However, an interaction like that can fester in your mind.

Try to remember a situation where you wanted to stand up for yourself more than anything, but you just couldn't. Now is your chance to reimagine that scene in a way that leaves you feeling more mentally satisfied and calm.

Pretend that you have the power of that moment back. Write down what you would say if you could look that person in the eye right now. What can you say to defend yourself without sinking to their level and resorting to put-downs?

After you have written down the script where you stand up for yourself, speak it aloud. Try to take back the power of that bad memory by expressing everything that should have been said. You deserved it then, and you deserve it now! Let this power soothe you.

Look at a Painting with New Eyes

❋

Some types of art can inspire and uplift you when you need some soothing. Turning to art for comfort is one way of celebrating its reason for existence. For this activity, choose a painting that you know you appreciate. It shouldn't be a favorite painting that you've seen a lot of times, but it should be one that you know can soothe you. If you own the original painting or it is on display locally, that's ideal. If you cannot go to the original painting, get a high-quality print.

Before you look at the painting, try to imagine that you are seeing it for the first time. Prepare to look at it without any expectations. Now look at the painting and immediately notice how it makes you feel and what you see first within the work of art. Look at it with a focus on its calming effect.

Gaze at the painting for at least thirty seconds. Look away from it. How did the painting make you feel?

Now look at the painting one more time with a goal of noticing something unusual you hadn't noticed before. It might be a detail in the background or a unique brushstroke. Look away, then gaze at it again, looking for something within the painting that makes you happy.

When you look at art with fresh eyes, you can appreciate it all over again. Play around with how you embrace this exercise and try to observe art that you love in all sorts of new ways.

Transform Judgmental Thoughts

Judgmental thoughts are inevitable—and they're not always bad. Sometimes we need to judge whether someone is likely going to be a good friend or whether they're an ethical person. However, a lot of judgmental thoughts are shallow and aren't the best use of your energy. Transforming your judgmental thoughts can help you relax and refocus your attention on what's really important.

Think of the last unjustly judgmental thought that came to your mind. Try to reimagine that judgmental thought through a more compassionate lens to invite some calm, rational ideas into the equation. For example, if you were criticizing someone's clothes, think about why they might be dressing that way, and how they might feel about themselves in those clothes. Would you really want to take away someone's joy if they felt good in an outfit that you simply didn't like? How would you feel if someone did that to you?

Instead, try to reframe that judgmental thought with kindness and compassion. Then work to make this a habit when judgmental thoughts come to mind.

Acknowledge and Validate Your Feelings

Validating your own feelings may sound like a simple concept, but it can be one of the most profoundly soothing actions you can take. The thoughts bouncing around in your head can seem chaotic, but naming and acknowledging them can give you a sense of control over them.

Start by naming each feeling you are having in this moment. It's okay to have more than one or to experience two that seem contradictory.

Now take this a step further. Talk about the feelings you are experiencing aloud to yourself. Then also validate those feelings. For example, if you are mad, tell yourself, "I am feeling mad right now. That can be a painful feeling. I understand why I am mad, though." Go on to explain aloud why you are mad. Acknowledge that this is a legitimate reason for being mad.

Be sure to nurture yourself as you acknowledge and validate your feelings. Tell yourself that although this feeling might be painful, it is temporary, like all feelings. Reiterate that feelings are neutral. They're not good or bad; they just exist. Also, remind yourself that all the feelings you have will pass. These reassuring statements can lull you into a calmer state of mind.

Release Responsibilities
That Are Not Your Own

If you're like most people, you take on responsibilities that aren't yours. That can start as a sincere and kind effort to help someone, but it can become unfair to you if the person doesn't resume their responsibilities. Release some of the mental pressure on yourself by letting go of at least one of those responsibilities.

Picture one of the unwanted burdens in your life that shouldn't be on your shoulders. Speak aloud or write down the reasons that it's not your responsibility. Now brainstorm exactly how you will release it. For example, you might call or email someone to say you aren't able to do tasks for them anymore. Envision yourself being brief but honest and open about why it's not your responsibility.

It's okay if you aren't ready or able to break from *all* your unwanted responsibilities yet. Still, make a plan for how you will release each one at a later date. Simply taking this concrete action can be soothing.

Create Comforting Statements

Sincere words of comfort can be profoundly soothing to the heart, mind, and body. However, the statements that comfort one person might make someone else feel anxious. So, it's important to take time to explore which specific words comfort you and acknowledge that you can give that comfort to yourself.

For this activity, say these simple statements to yourself. After each sentence you say, pause and try to really absorb the words. Then write down how it makes you feel.

* It's okay to feel anything that you're feeling.
* You are so brave to face this.
* This too shall pass.
* I'm sorry you are going through this.
* I love you.
* You are enough.
* Stand in your power.
* The best is yet to come.

Now star the sentences you like best and/or create one or two original statements that help you feel better. Finally, copy all the sentences that comforted you onto another sheet of paper or in your phone and keep the list where you can reread it the next time you're upset.

Reimagine a Place
of Extreme Beauty

Nature offers us beautiful and calming scenes every day. Think back to a place that truly wowed you with its beauty. Perhaps it was the view from the top of a hill after a long hike. Maybe it was the sight of a waterfall reflecting a rainbow of colors or the ocean as it sparkled in the sun.

Think of the thing you loved most about the place. Maybe it was the setting sun or the way you could smell the pine trees all around you. Close your eyes and imagine yourself back there. Focus on what you loved the most about the place. Make a mental note of all the sights, smells, and sounds you'd be experiencing.

Try to stay focused on this breathtaking place for five minutes, taking in all its beauty and joy. Then reflect on how this experience soothed you.

Balance the Scales

Having balance in life is important. If you give too much of yourself, you'll end up drained, both mentally and physically. In this exercise, you'll balance the scales and be sure you take care of yourself as well as you take care of others.

First, draw scales in the middle of a sheet of paper. Now think about how much you do for and give to others. Now think about how much you do for and give to yourself.

On one side of the paper, write down all the things you did for others this week. On the other side, record what you did for yourself. If you have been giving more to others, it's time to readjust your balance. You need to replenish yourself at least as much as you give to others.

Soothe yourself by writing down all the things that you commit to doing for yourself in the next few days. When you are kind to yourself, you empower yourself to be your kindest self for others.

Commit to Seeing Each Part of the Whole

When you're upset, it's all too easy to see only one side or part of something instead of the bigger picture. The new perspective you get when you step back and see a broader view can often reassure you.

To do this exercise, pick a large, interesting image from a magazine and tear it out. Now turn it over and cut it up into five or six different pieces. Mix the pieces all around so they are no longer in their proper order.

Turn one part over and look at it. What would you think of the image if this part of it was all you saw? How is it beautiful in and of itself?

Now turn over the next piece and look at the two pieces together. Can you instantly tell how they ultimately mesh? Is one part needed for the other to make sense or be beautiful?

Keep turning pieces over one at a time until you have all the pieces right-side up and have fitted them back together. Since they were rejoined, what is different about the image now?

Your perspective on a situation can have a huge impact on how it plays out. Defuse stress in your life by doing this exercise in your mind with something that's bothering you. Seeing how your piece fits with others can help bring you peace.

Recite a Poem

Reading the calming, lyrical, or profound words of a poem aloud can relax your mind and body. To try this out, choose a poem that comforts you. If you don't know a poem offhand, "The Summer Day" by Mary Oliver or a piece by Amanda Gorman might be a good choice. You can pick any poem at all, but it's probably best if it's no longer than a page.

Stand up and read the poem aloud. Try to spend a few minutes memorizing the first few lines. Now close your eyes and try to say them by heart.

Next, write the poem down (the process of writing something down can help you remember it). Reread the poem in your own handwriting a few times. Now close your eyes and see how much of the poem you can recite.

You may even want to record yourself reading it and then listen to the recording. Alternately, you can probably find a video of someone reading it on *YouTube*. Listen to the poem several times. Now try again to recite it by heart.

Now say the poem (or your favorite lines of it) aloud, content in the knowledge that you'll have it in your mind to soothe you any time you need it.

Organize a Drawer or Shelf

Being organized might seem challenging, but the effort is worth it. Living in a cluttered or disorganized space can increase your daily stress level if you're always tripping over clutter or misplacing your car keys. Today's exercise is all about organizing one small space that can have a big impact on how calm and soothed you feel.

Think about a messy drawer, shelf, or small part of a room that bothers you. Now consider what it would take to get it clean. Gather any necessary supplies, like cleaning spray, storage boxes, donation bags, or other organizational tools.

Commit to cleaning the drawer or shelf within half an hour. As you clean, think about how good it feels to relax in a pristine environment. Imagine your entire home fully organized. Reflect on what motivates you to get organized and stay that way. How is it calming to be organized?

Once you finish cleaning, take a long look at your newly organized space, and celebrate this small step in the right direction. Write down how it makes you feel comforted and inspired.

Finish a Jigsaw Puzzle

Putting together a puzzle can be a very peaceful, calming experience. Solving the puzzle can help you focus on a project that has a finite end, and it can almost be a form of meditation. There is a soothing repetitiveness to finding where one piece goes and moving on to the next.

Give your puzzle-solving experience an extra boost by turning on music that doesn't cause too much distraction (so your concentration can stay on the puzzle). Make sure you have a favorite beverage or snack on hand in case you need a quick break.

Plan to give yourself a reward after you have solved the puzzle (a walk outside in nature or a relaxing bubble bath). That can help motivate you to stay focused and on track as you strive to solve the puzzle. The prize can be part of the overall self-soothing experience too!

Promise to Make Positive Changes

Assessing what went wrong in a difficult situation and brainstorming ways to do things differently in the future can help you feel better. If you're upset, look at the root of the problem and assess which aspects of it are within your control. Now consider whether there are things you can do to prevent this unfortunate situation from reoccurring. For example, if you are upset because you missed an important deadline, think of five realistic changes you can implement in your life to meet your deadlines in the future.

Now make five reassuring and practical promises to yourself about those things you need to do. For example:

* I will buy a calendar today to help track work that's due.
* I will set up deadline reminders on my phone or computer.
* I will break down each job down into small, manageable tasks so I can complete my work on time.

Write your promises down. That way, they can soothe you and help you maintain accountability for keeping them.

Interview Yourself

People watch interviews to learn something new about the person being questioned. Why not try this with yourself and see what you can learn? Finding out more about why you are upset or anxious can help you get to the root of what's really bothering you.

Start by asking this complex question: How did you get to this point? Was there a triggering incident or perhaps cruel comment that made you feel bad? Was it something that stemmed from long-pent-up frustration? Continue asking logical follow-up questions so you can fully understand your feelings.

Now ask yourself how you can turn things around in the here and now. If you made a mistake, you might be able to find a way to fix it. Landing on a solution can immediately provide a salve and help you feel better. If you can't fix it, try to forgive yourself and move on. Lavish kindness on yourself as you explore some of the root causes of your suffering.

Interview Others

Self-soothing is extremely important, but you don't always have to do it completely alone. Don't be afraid to ask for help when you need it. You're likely to find that your loved ones will want to help, and it is marvelous to know you have a strong team in your corner when you need it.

Brainstorm a list of who you can reach out to for help in different areas of your life if you need it. Start the list by writing down the name, phone number, and/or email address of who you will turn to if you get down and need a friend in your corner to cheer you on.

Next, add notes for who would be the best contact in specific situations—for example, if you need help with a relationship, your career, and so on. Continue adding to the list with people you can turn to for help with every different aspect of your life.

Simply having this list close at hand can be comforting. The reassurance that your friends and loved ones will be there for you will arm you with a greater ability to self-soothe.

Create an Acrostic of a Comforting Word

An acrostic is a written work of art where the first letter of each word spells out a major important word. Choose a word that means a lot to you, then start the acrostic. For this example, let's use the word PEACE.

Start by writing the word vertically down a sheet of paper, then write a reassuring, empowering sentence that starts with each letter. For the word PEACE, you could write helpful statements as shown here:

* P: **P**utting myself first is okay.
* E: **E**verything is going to be all right.
* A: **A**ct with self-love even when I don't feel it.
* C: **C**hoose to do what makes me happy.
* E: **E**ach day has undiscovered joys in it.

An acrostic creation with an inspirational word is a simple but very effective tool for inviting calm back to your day. These powerful thoughts can help restore your sense of self when you feel unsure or anxious.

Start a New Project That Requires Concentration

Nothing unclutters the mind and pacifies the emotions at least temporarily like concentrating on something new and exciting. Taking your mind off your worries and diving into a project might be just what you need to reset your emotions.

Start a new project that requires concentration and focus. Choose an activity related to one of your hobbies so that it is fun and exciting, and that way it will also help keep your interest over time.

If you enjoy art, for example, you may choose to create a new series of paintings that will all somehow go together. You may spend a lot of time planning how each one makes sense within the series or how a color scheme will complement another one.

Whatever your project is, try to immerse yourself in it fully. If you can take the rest of the day off without negative consequences, try to do that and focus entirely on the new project for as long as it is making you happy and keeping your interest.

Set Up Friendly Boundaries

Boundaries in relationships get a bad reputation. The term makes people feel like it will distance them from those they love; however, the exact opposite is often true. Setting boundaries can bring people closer together in a way that is sustainable. Boundaries can be extremely soothing, too, as they can clarify expectations and establish comfort zones.

If you are upset because people don't treat you well, you may not realize that you have the power to change that in many situations. Although each person is completely responsible for their own behavior, there are often steps you can take to make things better for yourself.

Try to imagine setting up a friendly boundary with someone you love who sometimes doesn't treat you well or who demands too much from you. Write down who you're thinking of and what they do that's not acceptable. For example, maybe a friend regularly mocks you for one of your fears.

Next, write down how you can tell them what's bothering you and what you want instead. For example, you could let them know that mocking really hurts your feelings. You may want to tell them areas of your life where you don't mind some teasing. Reiterate what is and isn't acceptable for you.

Ultimately, the people you want in your life will appreciate your openness and bravery. It will free you both up to get what you need—and can deepen your relationship in the process.

Solve a Problem

What's more calming and confidence-inspiring than solving a problem? Of course, solving all the world's issues would be ideal. However, it's perfectly okay to think smaller and try to soothe yourself by solving just one problem today.

Think about your to-do list. What looms large and causes you worry but could be completed within fifteen minutes? Whatever it is, take on that problem and solve it. Do the thing you've been putting off. You'll find that annoying problem has been causing you more strife than it should have.

After you complete the task and solve the problem, reflect on how it feels. Allow yourself to be soothed by the feelings of relief and accomplishment that come from solving your own problem so efficiently once you made up your mind to do that. Let that empower you to approach other problems in your life in the same way.

Step Into a Fictional World

Sometimes the real world can be frustrating and unpleasant. When you need to be soothed quickly, try temporarily retreating into a fictional world instead. Close your eyes and think about your favorite fictional world. Whether it's an idyllic island, a medieval kingdom, or an unusual outpost in outer space, conjure it in your mind now and let that dream world start to soothe you.

Now envision what it would be like to truly live there. In what ways would your life be different or better?

Write down how you imagine your fictional world would play out. Do you want to bring along anyone from your real world into your fictional world? How might that person impact what goes on there?

Imagine all the wonderful possibilities of living in this fictional world. Savor the little pleasures of imagining all the cool things you'd get to do, see, and experience. Soothe yourself by letting your imagination delight and inspire you.

Count the Ways You Have Blessed Others

When you feel overwhelmed by your to-do list, it can feel like you never get enough tasks done. On the contrary, however, you have no doubt done so much for yourself and others. One thing that can provide an instant sense of relief and soothing calm is to make a list of all the ways that you have helped others.

Think of the impact your life has had on those around you and revel in the ways that you have brought joy to loved ones and helped others. Include anything that comes to mind. If you're not sure, ask your loved ones how you've helped them, and they'll probably happily tell you.

Next, consider the fact that you probably have had even more of a positive impact on people than this list shows. Savor the joy you are able to spread to those around you.

Choose a Talisman

A talisman is an object considered to bring good luck or fortune or even some type of magic to its owner. You can use a talisman to help you restore your sense of well-being anytime, anywhere. For example, you might want to hold a talisman for a few minutes before an important meeting, or look at it to cheer you up when you feel sad.

Your self-soothing talisman doesn't need to be something expensive or fancy. Choose an object that represents something that always makes you feel better. Think about some of the things that naturally have soothed you before—perhaps it was a hug from your dog. If that's your situation, you may want to choose a locket for your talisman and put your dog's photograph in it.

Your self-soothing talisman could also be a key that symbolizes your power to unlock positive feelings on your own. It could be a gemstone or an enamel pin with a design that resonates with you. A self-soothing talisman can really be anything at all that helps you get to a place of calm and relief.

Amplify Your Joy

When you feel upset, finding joy around you can change your mindset in a hurry. Think about the things in your day-to-day life that tend to spark the most joy inside you. Perhaps it is simple conversations about a favorite TV show with a coworker or the specialty coffee you enjoy every morning.

Pay attention to what brings you joy for the next twenty-four hours. If you start feeling joyful and aren't immediately aware of the cause, try to investigate it a bit to see what went right that led to this wonderful feeling. You may be surprised by some of the things that soothe you and bring you joy.

Once you have identified the things that make you happy and soothe you throughout the day, write about them and brainstorm how you can make them happen more often. Multiplying your joy-filled moments will lead to more peace and happiness throughout your day.

Take Mental Photographs

While living in the present is a great way to be mindful, the present moment doesn't always feel so great. For this self-soothing technique, you'll do a little time travel in your imagination and revisit a special time when you felt happy, peaceful, and blessed.

First, consider the happiest moments of your entire life. While you might have photos of those events, they might not capture what you remember as the most special parts of it.

When reflecting on your happiest experiences, take a mental photograph in your imagination. "Develop" this image by asking yourself these questions: What would that image look like? Who is present? What colors do you see? Why was this moment so amazing? What feelings does it evoke? Since this is a mental photograph, you can also use your senses to mentally immerse yourself in this special moment.

If you want, you could also write a description of each mental photograph you imagined so you can look back on it in the future when you need to be soothed.

Let Go of False Worries

Worrying steals so much joy from the current moment, and most of the things we worry about don't ever happen anyway. All worrying succeeds in doing is taking away your peace of mind in the current moment. For this exercise, you'll soothe yourself by acknowledging and dismissing these false worries.

Ponder the things that you're currently worrying about. List them one by one and ask yourself whether it's a true, legitimate concern or just you imagining an unlikely worst-case scenario. If it's a false worry, say aloud that you are letting it go and state why. Then do your best to let it go. It's okay to even wave goodbye to it.

Repeat this process until you have dismissed all your unnecessary worries. You will likely find a great sense of peace and calm as you free yourself from some of the stressors that don't need to cross your mind again.

Imagine an Ideal Future

The future is unknown, which is both exciting and a little unnerving. Embrace the positive potential of the years ahead of you to bring yourself a little peace today. For this exercise, imagine all the beautiful possibilities for our world.

Close your eyes and visualize a perfect world thirty years in the future. What are the things that would have to be eliminated for the future to be ideal for humanity? What has to be added?

Next, imagine what things will be like for *you* in thirty years. What kind of life do you want to be leading then? Soothe yourself by imagining all the wonderful things that can be happening in your life then.

Savor the happy feelings you have when you imagine how terrific things can be for you and the world at large. The best is yet to come!

Embrace Your Preferences

Knowing what you want is a good thing. It empowers you to go out and get it. It also helps you set goals and determine what you need to do to make those dreams come true. However, people who know what they want and are picky about getting it are often berated for being inflexible. Soothe yourself by giving yourself permission to enjoy your preferences and revel in that state of being.

Start with something simple. Write down what you want for breakfast. Make a list of the specific way that you want it. For example, if you want oatmeal, write down how you want the oats prepared, how you want it sweetened, the temperature you prefer, and other details.

Next, move on to something serious, like your relationships. What do you want from a friendship or romantic relationship?

Identifying your preferences is a powerful way to establish and own your identity. Don't apologize for who you are or what you like!

Choose a New Song for Inspiration

Sometimes it's helpful to expand your horizons and try something you wouldn't have otherwise done. This can be immensely soothing because it challenges your mind to get out of a stuck spot or downward spiral and instead engage with something new and exciting.

Choose to listen to a song today that is in a genre you usually ignore or a piece by an artist that you've never heard of before. Be sure to pick one that appeals to you for some reason, whether it's because of the subject matter or title. This should be a song that you are excited to hear!

Now listen to the song and write down all the terrific things about it. Look for ways that it can provide soothing and solace to you. Repeat the song a few times until your problems feel farther away than they were before.

Give Yourself Permission to Ask for More

Too often in life, people are shamed if they want more than they're given. That shouldn't be the case. You should be allowed to express your true wants, feelings, and desires. Soothe yourself today by giving yourself permission to ask for more of whatever you want.

Start by noticing what is going on with you in this moment. What would bring you the most relief in the moment? Do you want to talk to a friend but are afraid you might be disturbing them? Let go of that responsibility because it's up to your friend to decide whether they talk to you. If you want to talk to them, give them a call. By doing so, you are asking for their time, and that's okay. You deserve it!

Now think of what you'd like to eat. Are you given enough time to eat at lunch? If not, don't hesitate to ask for more so you get what you want. Asking for what you want is a way of soothing yourself by acknowledging and addressing the needs and desires you have.

Next, think of what you want to do. Do you avoid certain activities because other people in your group don't want to do them? If you want to go somewhere but your friends don't want to go, enjoy an outing by yourself.

When you're having a rough day, delight yourself by asking for *more* any time you want to do so. It's a freeing way to live!

Ignore Technology for the Day

Technology is an extremely important part of modern life, and many of us would feel totally lost without it. In fact, some aspects of technology probably help soothe you a lot of the time. Nevertheless, technology has its time and place, and it doesn't need to be ever-present in your life. Stepping back from technology for a day can have a relaxing effect on your body and mind.

Make a commitment to ignore technology for a day, or at least ignore it to the extent that is reasonable for you. If you have work or family responsibilities that you can't ignore for eight hours, that's understandable, but try to limit all unnecessary tech from your day.

Take a moment to assess how you feel after your time without technology. Do you feel more aware? Are you able to live more fully in the moment if you're not thinking about, say, posting about your experiences on social media?

Soothe yourself with the joy of breaking free of tech every once in a while. Taking some time to focus your attention on the here and now will allow your mind to feel re-centered, rebalanced, and rejuvenated.

Write a Soothing Poem

Poetry is an especially powerful art form. Through metaphors and painting mental images with words, poetry can deeply touch people's hearts. In this exercise, you are going to write a soothing poem yourself. If that idea doesn't seem instantly inspiring, don't worry: There's no wrong way to write poetry, and any creative expression is a great way to relax.

Start the poem with a strong expression of the last positive emotion that you can remember feeling. Next, follow that up with a metaphor about how things will go right today. It could be something very simple. For example, you can use buds on a flower to symbolize growth.

For the next part of the poem, write a sentence that you most need to hear. It might be an affirmation or a promise that you make yourself.

Conclude your poem with a few reasons why you love yourself. Soothe yourself by reading this personalized poem back to yourself. Let your own words and imagery remind you of the positive things happening in your life.

Set a Soothing Intention

Intentions are mental goals you set that empower you take responsibility for the way you experience life. Setting an intention to find ways to self-soothe will help you direct your energy toward that goal.

Start by simply declaring that you will soothe yourself whenever you need it. Next, identify why you need to soothe yourself and why it's important. Choose the tools that you are going to use to provide comfort. (That would include this book!)

Now refine your intention using the information you've brainstormed. For example, you might state, "I will prioritize soothing myself because I am worthy of love and respect. I will go for a walk when I need to because the physical activity helps my overall well-being." Personalize each intention using what soothes you the most.

Setting your intention shows that you are serious about taking care of yourself in a way that can make each day of your life better. There's no better way to show yourself love and respect than that!

Confront Your Fears

Fear holds us back in so many ways, seen and unseen. In this exercise, you'll confront your fears. Doing so can be soothing because after you confront and overcome those fears, they won't hold you back anymore.

Start by identifying a fear that holds you back. Write down what you would do if you weren't constrained by that fear. For example, maybe you would try out for a local orchestra if you weren't afraid of people judging you for not being good enough. Identify five of these primary fears, observing what you would do if you didn't have to deal with it.

Next, plan for how you can confront each fear. For example, if you are afraid of people's judgments, imagine yourself destroying any possible judgment by defending what you want to do. You should soon see that their judgments hold no true power.

You don't have to defeat all your fears at once, but taking the power back from them one at a time will decrease your worries, build your confidence, and encourage you to be more adventurous.

Meditate On What Soothes You

Meditation is one of the most popular self-soothing techniques in the world. Try meditating specifically on one thing that soothes you to comfort yourself in just a few minutes. What might your one thing be?

Get comfortable sitting in a relaxing spot where you will have peace and quiet. Start taking deep breaths. Inhale to the count of three, then exhale to the count of three. Then try to breathe at the same pace without counting.

Close your eyes and do a mental scan of your body to feel what's going on with it. Also acknowledge what is going on with you emotionally. Now turn your attention to focus on the comforting thing you identified earlier.

Worries will naturally come up once in a while—when that happens, simply acknowledge them and then return your focus to the one thing that is very soothing to you. Keep your focus on that as you continue to take deep breaths.

When you feel relaxed and comforted, close your eyes and continue to reflect for a few minutes before going about your day.

Generate a Self-Soothing Map

A map typically guides you around a certain physical location. For this exercise, you are going to create a special type of map that identifies and guides you to the easiest paths to self-soothing.

Start by identifying why you're upset. That will be your Point A. Now think of some of the best things in your life and what you cherish most. These happy places will be Point B on your map. Now let's consider what will get you from Point A to Point B.

Write down the things that truly soothe you enough to help transform how you're feeling. You may choose to write down the names of a couple of favorite films that can take you on the emotional journey you need to feel good. Alternatively, write down an activity that helps you feel better after only a few minutes.

Next, think about how you can access the soothing things that you identified. For example, if you find comfort in spending time with a parent, brainstorm some easy ways you can make that happen more often.

Now rest and assess your map. Let the creation of the map itself soothe you because it will be a tool you can use to find comfort more easily in your life. Revise and update it any time you'd like. It's your map, and you are in control!

Write a Thank-You Letter to Yourself

Thank-you letters are a lovely way to express gratitude in a personal, heartfelt way. When you do something nice for someone, it feels terrific when they let you know that your efforts were appreciated. In this activity, you'll turn the tables and write a thank-you letter to yourself! You no doubt have plenty to thank yourself for.

Start the letter by addressing yourself directly. Then write about one thing you've done lately for yourself that has really helped your overall healing and wellness journey. For example, you might express gratitude for your effort in soothing yourself when it's needed.

Next, describe how your life has changed for the better by the positive actions you've chosen to take. Express all the reasons why you appreciate what you've done for yourself.

Conclude your letter with details about how you want to continue to do great things for yourself. Make a promise. Then read over the letter and celebrate your effort and progress.

Reinterpret Old Photographs

Old photographs can help remind you of a wonderful time, but they can also sometimes be a source of sadness or shame. For this exercise, choose three photographs that contain an image of you that you've criticized. It's time to reinterpret those photos in a loving way. For example, if there is a photo where you wore a trendy outfit that now seems silly or had a bad perm in middle school, you can look at it through new, more loving eyes now.

Look at the first old photograph you've chosen. Now, instead of immediately criticizing who you were then, try to celebrate who you were in that moment. You were worthy of full love and acceptance just for being who you were!

Let self-love be the motivating force as you look at these old photographs. Look at the beautiful parts of yourself, then celebrate your past and present selves.

Create a Sign for Your Feelings

Many people look for signs that things are going their way. However, you don't have to wait for a metaphorical sign. Instead, create a literal sign to reassure yourself that you have every right to feel anything that comes to your heart and mind. A visual reminder that your feelings are valid and important is an empowering way to overcome fears and worries.

Get a piece of poster board or sturdy paper. Now decide what you want to tell yourself about your feelings. If you need reassurance that it's okay to express them, you might draw a green circle to signal the green light that means go and write some of your feelings around it. Alternatively, make a collage that inspires you to express yourself. This project can be as simple or as extravagant as you want it to be!

After you make your sign, hang it up where you can easily see it as a reminder to soothe yourself on an ongoing basis by expressing how you feel.

Celebrate the Ways
Others Love You

One of the most soothing forces in the world is love, and you can access the love others feel for you when you need to soothe yourself. You may not be able to call someone up when you need comfort at three a.m., but you can still experience their love any time in your mind.

Start by making a list of the ways that the people you love the most have shown you love recently. It can be something small like making you coffee in the morning, or something big like giving you an extravagant gift. Love can be expressed in a million different ways, and what matters here is that you choose ways that feel good and significant to you.

Next, focus on one special way that someone showed you love recently and dwell in the joy of how it made you feel by reliving what happened in your mind. Reclaim the feelings of happiness, gratitude, deep connection, and love that you felt in the actual moment. Let their action soothe you all over again now, or whenever you need it.

Live Mindfully

Mindfulness refers to living with a great awareness of the present moment. It is a mindset that keeps you grounded in the present, and it also helps ensure that you don't slip as easily into worries about the past or future as you otherwise might. Soothe yourself today by being more aware of all the good things that are happening in the here and now.

First, observe what is going on right now. You may have a project due, an incoming phone call, dinner cooking on the stovetop, or other urgent responsibilities running through your mind. Acknowledge that all of these things are in your life at this moment.

Now, try to set aside everything that's crossing your mind right now except for one thing you can immediately handle. You can handle only one task at a time, so focus entirely on that. Repeat this process for a few minutes until your mind has been freed up and soothed.

Envision White Light
All Around You

Simple meditations are a great way to calm your body and mind when you're feeling anxious or upset.

Start by getting comfortable. Now notice what you are seeing, smelling, hearing, and touching. What's the thing you are most aware of in this moment? After you acknowledge all that's going on with you in the moment, close your eyes, try to let go of it all, and focus completely on one thing: a soothing, healing white light that surrounds you.

With your eyes closed, visualize the white light enveloping your body. Breathe in, hold your breath, and then exhale slowly. Do this repeatedly as you imagine the light growing stronger. You may even imagine the light changing colors if that feels soothing to you. It can turn all the colors of the rainbow before returning to white.

Think about what the white light could do for you. How could it protect you? What do you need it to do? How can it most help you feel better? Imagine the white light doing whatever you most need it to do. Inhale and exhale slowly as you focus on the wonderful power of the white light.

Now imagine how you can provide a protective white light for yourself. You can take its soothing power around with you, and it can remind you to make self-protective choices.

Generate a Timeline of Joy

Joy isn't always easy to see when life is busy and stressful. However, when you look back over the details of your life, you are sure to find lots of moments when you experienced joy, even during extremely stressful periods.

For this activity, think back over the last month and write down a timeline of moments when you can remember feeling joy. For example, if you remember someone making you laugh during a tough time, write it down. Maybe you celebrated a birthday or the completion of a big work project. Look over your planner or calendar to see if any of the things you documented trigger a happy memory that you can write on your timeline.

This timeline of joy should provide comfort whenever you need reassurance that good moments are always there, even in the roughest of times, to provide solace.

Schedule Time to Daydream

Daydreaming is a pleasant, relaxing part of daily life for many people. When you daydream, the sky's the limit, and you can be anything and go anywhere you please. Daydreaming can be very soothing, too, because it reminds you that the positive possibilities for your life are endless.

If you're realizing that you haven't daydreamed in a while, look at your schedule for this week and schedule in time to daydream. That's right: Set aside time to just let your mind wander. Of course, daydreaming can also be spontaneous, but if you never seem to find the time to do it, you may need to *make* the time.

Whether you want to imagine an amazing trip, conjure up a romantic partner, or visualize yourself at the pinnacle of success, daydreaming is a powerful tool that's good for your mental well-being. Seeing happiness and fulfillment in your mind's eye is one step on the journey to seeing it in real life.

spirit

Whisper Your Sacred Words

Even if you don't consider yourself a spiritual person, you have words that are important to you. If you're not sure what yours are, ask yourself what matters the most to you. What is at the center of your heart? What makes you happiest? Who do you love the most?

Which words come to mind when you think of these things? Think beyond the names of loved ones or specifically naming a favorite sport. Instead, try to focus on the words that describe how these things make you think and feel. Some words might include *joy*, *hope*, *transformation*, *love*, or *gorgeous*. Don't judge the words that come to mind.

Make a mental list of what comes to your mind, then close your eyes and focus on those powerful words. Now whisper those words, getting a feel for how they sound and what it feels like to gently express them. Repeat them all at least ten times each. Allow them to soothe you.

Celebrate Your Accomplishments

Many of us are reluctant to focus on our own successes because doing so could be perceived as selfish or egotistic. On the contrary, celebrating your accomplishments is an important part of building self-worth and feeling spiritually content. Applauding yourself is also a great way to lift yourself up when you're feeling down.

In this exercise, you'll embrace tooting your own horn. Start by thinking of three things that you recently accomplished. They can be big or small. Learning a new skill is as important as a promotion when it comes to celebrating a step forward.

Now ask yourself how you want to celebrate each accomplishment. You can customize the celebration for each individual accomplishment. For example, you may want to reward yourself with leisure time after completing an intense work project. If you finished college, you may want to celebrate with something much bigger like a weekend getaway.

Each celebration should be special and fun for you. Be sure to congratulate yourself and reflect on all the challenges you overcame to achieve your goal.

Sit with an Animal

Companion animals like cats and dogs are sentient beings who are often very tuned in to the feelings of humans around them. Spending some time with an animal can help you forget your cares for a few moments and just relish their pure, unconditional love. If you have a pet, prepare to spend time with them. If you don't, volunteer at an animal rescue organization or a farm animal sanctuary in your community. Many people don't realize it, but some cows, turkeys, and pigs are also extremely intelligent companions.

Set aside at least ten minutes to just sit with the animal you've chosen. Make sure they have been recently fed and aren't in need of anything. Once the animal is comfortable and relaxed, you can get comfortable beside them. Observe how the animal relaxes in the moment.

Gently pet the animal and focus on how they react. Consider how their fur feels and observe how they are reacting to the physical connection. (Stop petting the animal if they seem uncomfortable.)

Try to mirror the animal and imagine life from their perspective. Think about what it must be like to be their height and rely on humans the way they do. Imagine what you can do to make their lives happier each day. What would you want someone to do for you if you were that animal?

Stay in the moment and observe the animal. Try to be as kind as possible in each moment you are with them. Then consider how you can be present with yourself and as kind as possible to yourself in each passing moment. Revel in how this soothes your whole being.

Imagine a New World

Sometimes escaping from your worries for a few minutes can be soothing. For this exercise, you'll visualize a new existence that's set up however you would like. What would you choose the world to be like if you could start a new one? Let your imagination soar with this concept. Focus on both the big picture and little details. You may choose a new color for the sky, the trees, and the ocean. On the other hand, maybe your world would have completely different terrain.

Start writing about this new world and how people would interact in it. In what ways could you make this new world less painful and more pleasurable? Consider all the ways that you could enjoy time with your loved ones in the new world.

Dwell in this imaginary world for as long as you'd like. Then you may want to start thinking about what you can do to add a bit of your imaginary world to the real one you live in.

Laugh from the Heart

There is a lot of truth to the saying "laughter is the best medicine." It may not really cure everything, but it's a great tool for self-soothing when you need to settle your overworked body, mind, and spirit.

Close your eyes and imagine a funny thing that happened to you when you were a little kid. (This shouldn't be a time when others laughed at you, but a moment you thought was genuinely funny.) Try to think of a memory of something that caused you to laugh in delight.

Once you have that in your mind, try to relive it and find the place inside that caused you to laugh when you were little. Think about how it felt to laugh before you worried about things like what others might think of your laughing at a certain joke or situation.

Now try to connect to that laughter and laugh out loud. Laugh deliberately. Pay attention to the physical sensations that laughter causes. Observe how laughing itself can improve your mood and soothe you.

Visualize a Treasure Chest of Comforts

If you know what brings you instant comfort, you can access it whenever you need it. One way to bring about a greater awareness of that for yourself is to visualize an imaginary treasure chest that is full of things that give you joy or solace. These should be things beyond physical treasures. Instead, consider intangible things that soothe you.

Close your eyes and think of one thing that would make you feel better right now. It might be something as simple as being told that you are strong and capable. Maybe it's the sound of a loved one's voice. Even the memory of the voice of someone who has passed away can be comforting. Try not to judge what comes to mind.

Make a list of all the things that come to mind as you try to visualize what you need to keep in an intangible chest to cheer you up when you need it. Revisit the list when you need reminders or a moment of peace.

Revel In a Rainbow of Candles

The flame of a candle can feel soothing and almost mesmerizing to look at. If you need to unwind after a hectic day or week, try sitting with several soy candles in a variety of colors. You could also use one or two scented candles to add an aromatherapy angle to this exercise.

Now turn out the lights in your room, light the candles, and observe the beauty of the rainbow of candles. Does the glow from the candles seem to change the color of the candle itself? How do the candles reflect on the walls and create interesting shadows?

Observe all the beauty of the candles and how they are making you feel. Does focusing on one flame for a minute allow you to briefly shut out some of your worries? Does breathing in your favorite scent help you relax?

Note: Be sure to stay safe as you relax with candles. Always blow them out before you leave a room or lie down.

Learn a New Artistic Skill

The arts feed the spirit in a way that few other tangible things can. Be kind to yourself and indulge your interests in the arts when possible. Think about an artistic skill you've always wanted to have and start learning it—any creative venture can become part of your self-soothing tool kit.

Maybe you always wanted to learn how to read music, paint with watercolors, create your own jewelry, make your own woodworking projects, or draw cartoons. Whatever your artistic preferences, decide to begin to learn something new.

Thanks to *YouTube*, online schools of all kinds, and other virtual opportunities, you don't have to wait weeks to start learning a new artistic skill—you can jump online today and get started figuring out what your first steps should be. After you learn some basics, you may want to seek expert instruction in person.

Spend ten minutes learning something about your new artistic skill right now, then decide how you'd like to take the next steps in your education.

Draw a Rainbow of Goals

Goals are an integral part of success for most people. They can also help you stay grounded, focus your energy, and motivate yourself to live your purpose and follow your passions. In this activity, you'll soothe yourself by looking at the wonderful, infinite possibilities ahead, and the knowledge that you are in control of your future.

Get a piece of paper or poster board and a pack of colorful markers. Draw a large rainbow that fills most of the space. Outline each part of the rainbow in a different color.

Close your eyes and think of your wildest dream— what you would do if you weren't held back by any financial, time, or logistical constraints. Write that dream on the outermost layer of the rainbow.

Now consider what else you would most want to do or accomplish, then write that on the next layer of the rainbow. Continue with this until you have the whole rainbow filled with your goals.

Read each goal aloud. Follow each dream by reassuring and soothing yourself with the phrase, "You can make your dreams come true."

Meditate On Your Personal Peace

Meditation is a well-known way to relax and re-center your body, mind, and spirit. For this exercise, you'll focus on what peace means to you and how you can find it.

To start, go to a quiet place in your home where you feel most comfortable. If others are at home, let them know that you need fifteen minutes without interruptions. Now, put a pillow on the floor and sit on it. Stretch and adjust your position until you feel comfortable.

Shut your eyes and start taking deep breaths. Be conscious of taking a deep breath in, holding it for a few seconds, and then releasing it. Repeat this over and over. As you do, start to think about what gives you a true sense of peace. There are no right or wrong answers here. What brings you a warm, peaceful feeling is what you should reflect on.

Open your eyes and focus all your thoughts on this peaceful feeling and what inspires it. Breathe in and close your eyes as you narrow your focus on it. Breathe out and open your eyes as you continue to focus. Do this several times in a row.

What does that peace inspire you to feel? Where do your thoughts go? Be aware of them and try to give all your focus to what that peace means to you.

After a few more moments of reflection, close your eyes and think about what you can do to bring some of your personal peace to fruition in this moment. Stand and stretch. Now try to take these peaceful feelings with you to soothe yourself through the rest of the day.

Wander and Wonder

Most of us only head out when we have somewhere to be at a certain time. That sort of scheduled, rushed travel is not usually relaxing. For this exercise, reintroduce a calm vibe to your travel by taking an hour or longer to wander around and appreciate what you see around you. This is more about a spiritual adventure than going somewhere for a reason. You may choose to wander in a busy downtown area, a mall that's great for people-watching, a quiet park, or a nearby beach. Any place that delights you will work. Bring along a journal to record some observations.

As you begin your wandering adventure, turn off your phone and other devices and place them in a pocket or bag, out of sight (and mind). As you wander, try to see the beauty and the wonder in all the things around you. Look at the world around you with rose-colored glasses. If you don't do this naturally, fake it for the moment.

Walk wherever you feel like going within the area you've chosen. After an hour or so, stop and write down all the wonderful things that came to your mind. Reflect on what you found most soothing and calming.

Act Like It's Your Last Day

Sometimes you don't know what you've got until it's gone. Though it may seem morbid, it can actually be soothing to look at your life as if you're about to pass away. This extreme perspective can force you to think about your priorities and appreciate all that you have to be grateful for. Today, stop and think about what you would do if you knew it was your last day on earth.

Ask yourself the following questions, then write down your answers. What activities, trips, or experiences would you make sure you do again? What would you want to try for the first time? What responsibilities would you abandon, and which ones would you keep? Who would you want to see and what would you say to them?

Now commit to living the next couple of hours as though it is your last day on earth. You don't have to do anything dramatic, but try to do something you really want to do with someone you want to be with.

When you're done, reflect on how looking at life from this perspective is eye-opening and soothing. Write about your observations if you like.

Create Your Own Safe Space

Your home should be a soothing haven for you to enjoy your life without the pressures of the world around you. But everyone has spots in their home that are stressful for some reason—a drab kitchen, a cluttered office—especially if it's shared with others. But you can still create a safe space within your home where you can always go to find comfort and feel safe from any triggering things that cause you to feel upset.

The best place for you to create a safe space may be in your bedroom, but you should choose the place that's best for you. A safe space can be as elaborate as a private backyard shed or as simple as a corner of your bedroom that's decorated with items that induce feelings of happiness.

Create your safe space and spend some time in it right away. Write down how it makes you feel and what you can add to it in the future. Keep changing and improving your safe space if you feel inspired to do so.

Paint Over the Pain

In this exercise, you'll release any stress, anger, or frustrations, then do your best to erase them—all via art. Get a canvas, a set of paintbrushes, and paints in some of your favorite colors. Now draw something ugly on the canvas. Whether you draw a jagged line or a detailed scene, tell yourself that it represents the pain or problem that is currently weighing you down.

Now paint in your favorite color all over the upsetting scene that you drew. Use a paintbrush to move the paint to cover the rest of the canvas. Let it dry. If it didn't cover your initial creation, paint over it again. Do this until the ugliness is completely covered by the paint.

Now you have a canvas with a blank slate except for the coloring you chose. Think about all the things that you can now add to the painting—perhaps something happy or hopeful. You can follow the same process with your pain in the real world—identify it, then try to turn it into something positive.

Be Inspired

No matter how stressful a day might be, it can be comforting to realize that it will not last forever. No matter how insurmountable a problem may seem, it can be soothing to read about people who have overcome that problem—or even worse problems.

Set aside some time to read a biography or an article about someone who has overcome something like a dilemma that's worrying you. Also choose to read about someone you personally admire and aspire to be like.

As you read the story you've chosen, consider taking notes on the parts of it that resonate with you. Perhaps the hero made a choice that will inspire you to take a certain direction in your own life. Jot down notes about anything that inspires you.

Ultimately, in addition to being comforting, these stories can also offer insights into how successful people overcame a problem. Strong guides who lead the way are an important part of nearly any spiritual practice, and you can strengthen your own spirituality by choosing to follow in the path of heroes you admire.

Declare Yourself Radically Free

Do you ever feel like you are tethered to misery because you're being kept from doing what you really want to do, or you can't express what you really want to say? Finding personal freedom is a lifelong goal for some people, but any steps you take on that journey will provide a measure of solace and joy.

When you have a few private moments at home, give yourself full permission to be free to say anything you want. While you shouldn't call, text, or email others within this heightened state of freedom, you should express anything that comes to your mind while you're enjoying this alone time.

Now *do* what you most want to be doing in this moment. Of course, you don't want to do anything that could have a negative impact on others. Otherwise, let your imagination soar. If you want to dance to the music no one else in your house likes, go for it. Focus on the feeling that comes from freeing up areas that normally feel controlled.

Doing what you want to do in the moment can soothe you and help you feel like you're radically free! You may want to repeat this exercise regularly.

Try Paced Breathing

Paced breathing is not only extremely soothing; it can also help your mind, body, and spirit feel more connected since it helps you stay aware and present in the moment.

Start by breathing in as you count four seconds, then exhale for six seconds. If you have a ticking clock in the room, you may imagine yourself breathing rhythmically with that. Paced breathing can almost feel a bit musical as you try to count and stay at a certain pace.

Continue this paced breathing pattern, inhaling for four seconds, then exhaling for six seconds. You may turn on a song that can help you keep count, or you may choose to think about a pleasant image that helps you stay focused as you count.

Paced breathing can easily become a habit that helps you feel better anytime and anywhere you need it. Breathing patterns have a big impact on both your physical and mental well-being.

Examine Interesting Patterns

Interrupting the nonstop chatter in your head is an important first step to soothing yourself. Looking at detailed patterns can be an interesting way of shifting your attention from your worries to something relaxing.

For this exercise, you will focus on patterns and how they have an impact on how you feel. Pull up images of interesting patterns on your computer. These could be from old tapestries at museums, bathroom tile, wallpaper, or modern art.

Examine the patterns and observe how they make you feel. If people hung these pieces of art or decor in their homes, how do you think it would make them feel? What were they hoping to convey to guests? Can art made only of a pattern stand for something deep? Why and how?

Thinking about your feelings as you observe patterns is a great way to notice what's on your mind. Follow the various lines and curves with your eyes as you let your spirit follow its own path forward.

Do Something You're Great At

Being good at something likely reinforces your affinity for the activity and can inspire other good feelings too. In fact, it can be extremely soothing to allow yourself to excel at something. You build confidence and boost your spirit, and the activity may even bring joy to others as well as yourself.

Set aside an hour to focus on something you enjoy doing that you're also great at. This could be anything from coaching Little League to painting a canvas to dancing. Any activity works if it's something you excel in and like to do.

After the hour is up, take a moment to relax and reflect on how the activity made you feel. Write down how it was soothing and how it made you feel better.

Spend Time Stargazing

Most of us spend little time outdoors at night, but the immense night sky can help your spirit find a new perspective on problems that seem to loom large.

Plan to do this exercise on a clear night in your yard or another safe outdoor area near your home. Start by stepping outside and observing what you see and hear. Do you feel connected to this outdoor world? What do you find immediately comforting here? Take some deep breaths.

Look up at the stars and ask yourself how connected you feel to the other galaxies beyond our own. Remind yourself of the significance of every breathing being. Every living thing impacts other things in the universe. Soothe yourself by envisioning your own power in the world.

Now stretch your arms as high as you can. Pretend you are reaching for the stars in the sky. Imagine what a different world it would be if we could actually reach the stars. Would you prefer it that way? Stretch your body and embrace being a part of both the earth and sky.

Meditate On Letting Go

Letting go can be spiritually freeing. Try this simple meditation to calm down and soothe yourself when you are thinking about letting go of something in your life.

Find a comfortable place where you're not likely to be disturbed. Sit down and relax as best you can. Set a timer for five minutes so that you know you are on a time limit and won't need to focus for long.

Now close your eyes. Inhale deeply, then exhale deeply. As you inhale, think of what you need to release, then envision letting it go as you exhale. Do this repeatedly. As you do so, take an awareness of your body. Are you feeling stress or pain anywhere? What is this making you think and feel? Continue to breathe deeply and try to also let go of each negative feeling as you exhale.

When the timer goes off, observe what you are thinking and feeling. If you feel like you need to further explore your meditation, you may choose to set the timer again and continue.

Make a Collage of Hope

Making a collage is a creative, low-pressure way to mentally envision the things you aspire to achieve and attain in your life. When you need to relax, try making a collage of hope to celebrate the great possibilities that lie ahead for your future.

Choose a large piece of colored cardboard or poster paper. Gather old magazines, beat-up picture books, old fabric scraps, glue, and some markers.

Go through the magazines, picture books, and scraps. Cut out images that convey the things you aspire to achieve or have in the next couple of years. The pictures don't all have to be on the nose in how they relate to your aspirations—a suitcase could represent a trip you want to take if you don't have an image of a particular location.

When you've cut everything out, choose one main image to represent hope right in the middle of your collage. It's a good idea to choose a large image, but you can pick any visuals that convey your number one priority.

Now place your other visuals in a creative collage in any way you'd like. Arrange the images loosely at first so you can rearrange as necessary, then glue everything down when you're happy with the look and feel.

When it's done, hang the collage in a very visible spot so that you can regularly be inspired to keep pursuing your dreams. Let it soothe you and be a reminder that the best is yet to come.

Think about Your Favorite Things

Like Julie Andrews sings in *The Sound of Music,* thinking about your favorite things can be comforting in difficult times. In this exercise, you'll list what your favorite things are so you can call them to mind to soothe yourself whenever you need it.

Get several sheets of paper. At the top of each sheet of paper, list one of these headings with the word "favorite" in front of it: Songs, Movies, Singers or Bands, TV Shows, Scents, Places, Things to Do, Restaurants, and Books. Now consider any other topics you'd like to cover and write them at the top of new pages.

Now list your favorite things in each category. Focus on each one as you write it down, taking time to savor the happy feelings it brings. If you can't think of any more for a certain category, go to the next page, and you can always come back and add more later.

Once you complete your lists, keep them handy. Start choosing one thing from a list to enjoy any time you need to soothe yourself.

Set Aside a Half Day for Fun

Think about the last time you had fun for hours. How long ago was that? If you're feeling overwhelmed, anxious, or upset, spending a day doing a bunch of fun things might help you reclaim some inner peace and joy.

Take a half day off work and postpone as many responsibilities as you can, then start planning your perfect fun afternoon. Whether you decide to watch a movie, take a dance class, or go on a long hike, give yourself the gift of fun. At the end of the activity, see if you were able to relax, find a new perspective, or at least forget your troubles for a while.

Fun is naturally soothing, so embrace that you can create it for yourself by doing things that make you happy. Try to commit to adding joyous things to your schedule on a regular basis.

Give Yourself a Graduation

A graduation is usually celebrated as the end of many years of studying—yet the term *commencement* means "a new start." Try celebrating something important in your life that's recently come to an end, and soothe yourself both with pride in your past accomplishments and hope for your bright future. Your spiritual self will relish this important rite of passage.

Celebrate when something significant comes to an end in your life by giving yourself a graduation from it. The ceremony can help you celebrate the end and begin to plan your next steps. You can hold a graduation for an event as serious and complex as a divorce, or as happy and light as the ending of a TV show you love.

You can mark the occasion in any way you choose. Perhaps you want to read aloud a commencement address about how you feel about this ending. You may choose to wear a hat and throw it in the air. Just be sure to also add a component that commemorates this moment as the beginning of a new phase.

Brainstorm a Resolution of Joy

Resolutions aren't just for New Year's Eve—you can make a resolution any time you want. The idea is to simply make a decision to do or not do something. Resolve to start doing something today that will bring you joy and soothe your spirit.

If you don't immediately know what to choose, reflect on the first thing that comes to your mind that would bring you immense joy. What draws you to it? Why haven't you been doing it already? If you truly want to do it, make it a resolution, and overcome obstacles so you can claim that happiness.

After one day of sticking to your new resolution, reflect on how it makes you feel. Does it soothe you and give you a sense of accomplishment? If you are happy that you made the resolution, commit to keeping it on a long-term basis and revel in the joy it brings.

Release Your Control
for the Moment

All humans want to feel a sense of control over their lives. But putting all your energy into trying to control everything can lead to exhaustion and frustration, and might not even change the outcome anyway. In this exercise, you'll experiment with releasing control and enjoying the freedom that can provide your body, mind, and spirit.

Think of something in your life that you are trying very hard to control. Maybe it's the grades that you are making in grad school or whether a crush will end up liking you. While you can certainly impact some aspects of these situations, you don't want to get so caught up in what you want the result to be that you miss the journey along the way.

For now, try to let go of your control. Close your eyes and imagine how freeing it would be if you were no longer trying so hard to control every little thing. For example, tell yourself that you will work hard and study, and whatever grades you get, you get. Or simply be yourself, and if that crush likes you for you, great. Visualize that control slipping from your hands and taking your stress and anxiety with it.

Focus On Technique

Technique is the method or way of carrying out a specific task. Whether it's the specific way you dance, the construction tools you use, or your workout regimen, everyone has techniques they use every day. For this activity, think of one of your hobbies and commit to trying a new technique to mix things up and dedicate your mind to learning something new. Switching things up with a hobby can keep your mind off your worries as you live in the moment, letting your mind focus only on technique.

Once you decide on a technique you could change, research a couple other options, then choose which one to try. Remind yourself that this new skill likely won't feel as easy as your old, familiar one, but that's okay. Training your brain to do new things helps boost creativity and flexibility. Don't aim for perfection; just focus on doing the technique as best you can.

When you're done, reflect on how soothing it can be to simply focus on a new-to-you technique. You might even decide to use this technique (or certain aspects of it) going forward.

Voice Your Gratitude

A thankful heart has been said to be one of the ultimate spiritual practices. There's something about living in a state of gratitude that can invigorate the spirit, and you just might find that it's easier than it seems to find things that make you feel thankful. That, in turn, can be instantly soothing and joy-inducing.

Start by closing your eyes and thinking of something nice that happened today. It should be something that makes you feel thankful. If nothing comes to mind, think about something positive that happened yesterday.

Once you have the object of gratitude clearly in your mind, start talking aloud about all the things that are so terrific about it. If you believe in God or a higher power, thank God directly for the experience. Express all the reasons that you are grateful for the experience or object. Try not to judge the words that come to mind; simply express how you feel.

After you have fully expressed your gratitude, close your eyes and think about all the positive possibilities for such things in the future.

Practice Self-Love

Self-love is a cornerstone of effective self-soothing. Loving yourself helps you realize that you truly deserve peace and happiness. Ideally, you already feel a lot of love for yourself. It's okay if you don't, though. This exercise will help you identify and celebrate all the amazing parts of yourself.

Start by trying to accept yourself just as you are. Most people are their own worst critics. However, it's important to acknowledge that you are worthy of love just as you are. If you struggle to love yourself, write down your responses to this statement: "I would love myself if not for…"

Now look at the reasons you've listed. You deserve your own love even with the faults that you have. Tell yourself that. Think of what you would tell a friend who tried to say they didn't deserve love because of those things. You'd likely insist the opposite, and remind them they are perfect just as they are. Talk to yourself with that type of affection and grace.

Now write down all the things you love about yourself. Keep writing as long as you feel inspired to do so. Focus on these deep feelings of love you have for yourself and let them soothe you.

Deepen Your Relationships

One surprising way to soothe yourself is to deepen the connections you have to others. Everyone needs fulfilling relationships in their lives, and growing closer to some important people can make you feel strong, resilient, and optimistic—in other words, calm and ready to face and overcome any challenge.

First, identify one thing that you can do to enhance your primary relationship. Whether you are closest to a friend, a parent, a sibling, a child, or a partner, think about a way that you can make the relationship better. That might be giving more or giving less, communicating more clearly, or expressing your love in a new way. Then take that action or plan to do so.

Do the same for a handful of other important people in your life. Take a simple action like writing a thank-you note for something they did or calling them to express your affection. Consider what the relationship needs and try to fulfill that need.

On the other hand, if you need something from these relationships, ask for it. This is about both giving and receiving.

Next, look at your relationship with yourself. That's the longest and most important relationship you will have, and it's also the one that may evolve the most over time. Reflect on how you can better connect with yourself and how you can better take care of yourself. Finally, write yourself a letter that outlines any actions you will take to secure, improve, or strengthen your relationship with yourself.

Encourage Wonder

We most often associate wonder with childhood—but adults shouldn't be left out of this magical sensation! Life is more pleasurable when we learn to see and appreciate the inexplicable beauty and goodness that's out there. Soothe yourself by embracing wonder in your own part of the world and encouraging more of it.

Start by packing a notebook and going for a walk or a drive. Try to be hyperaware of your surroundings and take a new route you've never been on, if possible. Look for the beauty in the day. Stop your car or stop walking when you come to a scenic spot. It can simply be a park with green grass, a mural in the city, or a building with architecture you admire.

Take notes on everything special about it. When you think you've gotten it all down, try to look at it with new eyes and observe even more wonder.

Continue the process, stopping at a different sort of place and observing the wonder there. Try to keep this mindset in your everyday life, pausing on the way to lunch to appreciate talented street performers or waking up early to catch a magnificent sunrise. Soothe yourself with all that's splendid around you, then consider sharing your thoughts about it on social media. Spread the joy around!

Try Something You Fear

Fear certainly has a practical evolutionary purpose. However, nowadays it is often misplaced, and it can hold you back from things you truly want to do. Soothe yourself and free your spirit by facing one of your fears.

Think about something you would do if you weren't afraid. It doesn't have to be something big or dangerous. It could be as simple as calling a friend to mend a long-ago quarrel or posting a selfie on social media.

As you face the fear, consider all the reasons that you have for being afraid. Dismiss the ones that are clearly unfounded. If you have legitimate reasons, consider the risks. If you think it's worth it, now is the time to face it.

Do what you fear, then write about your experience. Did you feel triumphant and proud? No matter what happened, heap praise on yourself for facing your fear and be soothed by this life triumph.

Plant Metaphoric Seeds

Planning for the future isn't a perfect science. You can set goals and imagine what might happen, but ultimately you need to take a leap of faith and continue living to see what transpires. Things might turn out just as you pictured, or a totally different outcome might surprise and delight you. This exercise is all about embracing the leap of faith.

People often plant flowers several months before they expect them to bloom, or sometimes they plant a mix of seeds and aren't sure which ones will flourish. Think of planning something terrific in your life like planting these seeds and waiting for flowers to bloom.

Brainstorm about the things you want to bring to fruition, then jot down what it will take to make each one happen. If they are quick, easy things to do, start doing them. Otherwise, simply make a commitment and plan when you will do them.

Then sit back and savor the joy of planting these metaphoric seeds. Reflect on how the resulting flowers will color your world in one beautiful way or another in the future.

Write a Movie Synopsis
of Your Ideal Life

Your imagination has an incredible power to bring your spirit the peace and happiness it craves and deserves. Let it soar with this fun exercise in dreaming…and escapism.

Before you start writing, look at some of the synopses of your favorite movies. They are usually a few sentences long and provide the basic plot framework without giving away the ending.

After reading a few examples, start thinking about what the perfect movie synopsis for your ideal life would be. Starting from this moment on, what do you want to happen? From love to career, think big and consider what you truly want.

Now read it aloud and make any necessary edits. Which actors would you want to play you and other supporting characters?

Reflect on this process and on a simple awareness that anything you wrote is possible. Revel in the possibilities for your future and let them soothe you in this moment.

Create a Circle of Gratitude

Gratitude is a powerful healing force. Studies have shown how keeping a gratitude journal each day can help improve your mental health and soothe your spirit.

For this exercise, start by gathering a pen and a stack of index cards. They can be plain, colorful, decorative, or any design you like.

Find a comfortable spot on the floor where you have room to spread out. Take one of the cards and write down the first thing that comes to your mind when you start counting your blessings. Then put the card down on the floor. Now take another index card and write something else you are thankful for, then set that card beside the other one.

Continue the process, forming a circle with the cards. Continue this until you create an entire circle of gratitude around where you are sitting on the floor.

Now look around at how the words reflect the things in your life that spark gratitude. The circle represents how your blessings can metaphorically encircle you and help you feel safe, happy, and calm.

Celebrate Your Spiritual Habits

Some people have very well-defined religious or spiritual practices based in one system or approach. But many other people pick and choose preferences from a variety of different sources. And both methods are perfectly okay! Doing whatever makes you feel fulfilled, hopeful, and blessed will undoubtedly improve your mental, spiritual, and physical well-being.

Write down what your special spiritual habits or unique preferences are. You might attend organized group services once a week. Or perhaps you have a natural affinity for certain animals and feel like you connect with them in an almost spiritual way. Maybe you write your own meaningful prayers or consider your weekly bubble bath to be kind of like a ritual, with candles and scents.

Now think of how this habit has protected you from harm, soothed you, helped someone else, or was otherwise beneficial to you. After identifying this, write down why you are thankful for that particular preference. If you couldn't discern how the habit is beneficial, think about whether you really like it. If you don't, change it. Then celebrate the peace of mind and serenity of your acceptance.

Bury the Past

Everybody has something in their past that they need to release. This could be something very small, or it might be something that looms large in your life. Whatever it is, this exercise will be both soothing and healing as you will finally let it go.

Start by writing down whatever it is you want to move past. You might write just a single word to remind you of it, or you could write something in-depth about the experience. When you're done, tear up the piece of paper.

Next, go into your backyard (or use a large potted plant if you don't have a yard) and dig into the dirt. You can use a shovel or, if you're feeling adventurous, just dig in with your hands or another object. Just dig deep enough to bury the scraps of paper.

As you cover the paper with dirt, promise yourself that you are releasing this burden from your body, mind, and spirit. Let the release soothe you as you bury the symbol of the past and leave it behind.

Identify Your Joyful Triggers

❁

You have probably seen trigger warnings online before articles and posts. They can help people who have been through a trauma avoid being brought to a harmful place because something is such a strong reminder of it.

Just as something can be a negative trigger, though, you can also have a positive trigger that makes your whole self feel better. These positive influences can relax your muscles, quiet your mind, and give your spirit new life. This exercise will help you learn to soothe and uplift yourself with joyful triggers.

Consider the last time you felt down. What cheered you up quickly? Is it something you can turn to again? Whether it was watching a certain movie or the smell of a certain candle, you may be able to identify something that provides instant comfort. That's a joyful trigger.

Make a list of these positive triggers in your phone. That way, they're easily accessible during difficult times. Try to keep the list updated as you find new ideas or retire old ones.

Step Outside Your Comfort Zone

Most of us do the same things every day, and there can be comfort in routine. But it can also be soothing to try something different. You might build confidence, learn something new, or enjoy a novel experience.

Choose a low-stakes situation and do the opposite of what you would normally do. For example, if you normally drive around a parking lot to find a spot close to the entrance, try grabbing an easy spot far from where you need to go instead, then walking. Then choose another low-stakes situation and repeat the process, trying a new way of doing things.

It is incredibly soothing to discover that you have the power to change the way you've done things before. It's never too late to look at life differently and broaden your horizons.

Give a Soothing Sermon

Many people cringe when they hear the word "sermon" because they envision angry preachers yelling fire-and-brimstone warnings about eternal damnation. However, a sermon is simply a talk on a moral topic, and it doesn't need to be negative or religious at all. Rather than scare anyone, you can use a sermon to soothe yourself.

Start by writing the sermon you need to hear. Consider a moral or spiritual concern in your life or think about a topic that's important to you—these would be good subjects to write about.

Next, choose a quote or verse that's meaningful and relevant to the point you want to make. Now think of a few basic points you want to make in support of that. These should tie in with the overall message you want to communicate.

Now expand on your message by explaining how it applies to your own life and circumstances. How can you help and reassure yourself with this message? What hope do you have to offer? Speak from your heart. You don't have to write a long sermon. Try to stay focused on the topic at hand and don't write more than a page or two.

When you're done, read the sermon aloud to yourself, pausing to take in the words that you've written and the message that you're conveying to yourself. Listen attentively to what you're saying and let the words soothe and inspire you. Also savor the power you have to comfort yourself with words and ideas already present inside you.

Practice Self-Compassion

For many of us, it's much easier to have compassion for others than it is to have it for ourselves. However, you need your compassion more than anyone else in the world does, so it's important to learn to give it to yourself. Treating yourself with love and respect is truly spiritually rewarding and soothing.

Start by thinking of a recent time that you really needed attention, validation, or forgiveness. Were you ever vulnerable to someone who didn't honor those feelings in the way you needed? What do you wish that person had done?

That's what you can do for yourself next time. For example, if you need to be forgiven for a mistake you made, offer that to yourself. If you have to "fake it until you make it," that's okay. Go through the motions of trying to offer compassion to yourself. Make sure your words, tone, and body language are gentle and considerate, and really try to mean what you say and do.

Treating yourself with compassion might take some practice if it hasn't been your habit in the past. Be gentle with yourself as you learn and improve.

Change One Thing

Your perception might lead you to feel one way about a situation…but what if one little thing was different? When you experience a shift in what you think you know, you can soothe yourself when you realize things aren't as bad as you thought, or that maybe there is a solution after all. After all, first impressions can be altered when you get more information.

For this exercise, think of a situation that's bothering you. What if you made one small change to it? For example, if your job feels too stressful, could you ask your boss if you could take one project off your plate? Or if you are overwhelmed with household chores, could you ask a family member to do one chore regularly?

You'll soon see that one simple change can impact your whole mindset. Now think of all the stressful situations in your life. If you changed one small thing about each, wouldn't that change everything? Allow yourself to be soothed by the realization that you need to look more closely at each situation.

Detox Your Spirit

The human spirit receives a lot of toxic information, negative feedback, and outright lies each day. It can be hard to keep hope and joy thriving within if you are exposed to a lot of negativity from the people or circumstances around you. Soothe yourself by detoxing from some of the harmful things that threaten your spiritual well-being.

First, try to be very aware of how people make you feel. Observe how you feel after each encounter with people you have today. Write down whether you felt better or worse after seeing them. If there is no practical explanation for feeling bad after the encounter, try to eliminate interacting with that person for twenty-four hours and see how you feel.

Now look at how you interact with the world around you. Are you following social media channels that regularly bring you down? Is your office space or home gloomy or discouraging? Adjust your habits or environment to get rid of some of that negativity. Soothe yourself with kindness as you detox from the world's harm to your spirit.

Look at Yourself from Another's Point of View

We're often our own worst critics—your friends, family, and loved ones probably think better of you than you think of yourself. If you need to boost your spirit, ask someone to write a one-paragraph description of you. Tell them to be honest but request that they accentuate the positive.

Now, go somewhere private and read what they wrote aloud. How does it make you feel? If it makes you want to leap for joy, do just that! If it makes you blush or glow, savor that feeling. If it makes you feel tired or overwhelmed, honor those feelings too. Lie down if you need to do so.

Now read their description again and try to imagine yourself as the other person looking at you. Can you see why they came up with the description that they did? Does any part of it make you uncomfortable? Do you trust that everything they said was true? Try to let go of any doubts and allow yourself to be soothed by the compliments and praise.

Welcome Unexpected Twists

Life is full of surprises. We all must learn to expect the unexpected if we're not going to be continually flustered by life. The key is to embrace the twists and turns that life takes you on, and try to look forward to any blessings you find in them.

For this activity, consider the last time something unexpected happened to you. Now think of what happened next. The consequences of a flat tire, for example, might have initially been that you missed a concert, but you also ended up meeting someone during that experience who became a friend for life. Not every twist looks good at first. Make a list of at least five positive outcomes from unexpected happenings.

Now, when you look to the future, soothe yourself with the reassurance that life's surprises often lead to great experiences. The life you might choose for yourself usually isn't nearly as colorful and full as the one that happens, so you might as well bring a positive outlook and enjoy the journey.

Write Five Letters

People too often leave important things unexpressed in life, and that often leads to regrets, long-held grudges, and unnecessary rifts that impact your overall well-being on a very deep level. It can be helpful and soothing to express how you feel, even if you don't communicate those feelings directly to the people who caused them.

Think about the people in your life who inspire strong feelings in you. Now sit down and write five short letters to these people about how they make you feel. For example, you may write a thank-you letter, a love letter, a letter that expresses pure rage about something that's still unresolved, a letter of apology, a whimsical letter about your hopes for the future, and any other letter that touches upon a strong feeling you have.

Each letter can be as long or as short as you want. When you've finished the letters, you can set them aside or dispose of them. Give them to the person only if you feel a strong need to do so. Getting these feelings off your chest can lift a heavy burden off your spirit even if you don't send the letters.

Embrace Your Mistakes

Nobody wants to make mistakes—but we all make plenty of them, so we might as well learn how to deal with them. When mistakes are your fault, it's good practice to apologize for them, but it's not a good idea to dwell on them. Reliving mistakes and continually punishing yourself for them only leads to physical stress, feelings of low self-worth, and spiritual discomfort. Soothe yourself by taking on a new attitude about your mistakes.

Consider how a mistake that you made had a positive outcome. For example, if you accidentally took a wrong turn but wound up discovering a scenic route, that would be a pleasant mistake. Marvel at how your mistake ended up helping you and others. After all, maybe you then shared the scenic route with others.

Now consider how a mistake brought you closer together with someone. If you own up to your mistakes and take responsibility for them, you may find that your mistakes help you get closer to your loved ones. Then reflect on how you learned from a past mistake and never made it again, therefore ultimately growing as a person. Soothe yourself by reminding yourself that it's okay to make mistakes now and in the future—and that they often have a positive outcome when all is said and done.

Listen to an Inspirational Speech

Sometimes self-soothing is all about knowing which tools are on hand to lift yourself up when you can't do it entirely on your own. When you're feeling down, one way you might lift yourself up is to listen to an inspirational speech.

You may choose an emotionally significant speech from heroes of the past or opt for something contemporary. It may simply be a social media video that's made to inspire a quick smile.

Choose a speech, then commit to listening to it with an open mind. Take in the speaker's words and try to imagine how they wanted you to perceive them. Do you agree with them? Allow yourself to find comfort in the speaker's words if you feel they are true.

Once you are done listening to the speech, write a short reaction to it. Simply write down how you would respond to the speech if it was a dialogue. Thank the speaker for how their words soothed you, and continue on with your day, enjoying the motivation or optimism that the speech provided.

Be of Service to Others

When things feel bleak, taking action to change them can feel empowering and soothing. So, today, dedicate yourself to taking a single action to change something you think should be different.

Sit down with a blank notebook. Jot down anything you can do to make the world a better place. For example, if you are frustrated by trash in your neighborhood, you could grab gloves and a trash bag and clean things up. If you have a cause that's near and dear to your heart, join a local group that's working for that cause and donate your time or money.

After you've volunteered your time, use the notebook to record what you chose to do and how it made you feel. Making the world a better place a little bit at a time is a great way to feel a strong sense of spiritual community with the rest of our planet.

Start Caring for You!

Pick Up or Download Your Copies Today!